PENGUIN BOOKS

BBC BOOKS

GREAT RAILWAY JOURNEYS

Clive Anderson is a London barrister and comedy writer who hosts his own television talk show. He has also presented a range of programmes featuring improvisation, politics and the Bayeux Tapestry.

Natalia Makarova, the internationally acclaimed prima ballerina, has danced all the great classical roles and has staged many productions, including *La Bayadère*. In addition to her dance awards, she has won both the Tony and the Olivier awards for Best Actress and has published *A Dance Autobiography*.

Rian Malan is an Afrikaner who fled his homeland in South Africa in 1977 to live in America. He returned eight years later and wrote the bestselling *My Traitor's Heart*. He now works as a reporter in South Africa.

Michael Palin's comic reputation was established by *Monty Python's Flying Circus*. His work includes several films, among them *A Fish Called Wanda*, the television series *Around the World in 80 Days* and *Pole to Pole* and the accompanying bestselling books.

Lisa St Aubin de Terán was born in London. She married when she was sixteen and for seven years managed a sugar plantation in Venezuela. She is the author of seven novels, a volume of poetry, a collection of short stories and a book of memoirs. She now lives in Italy.

Mark Tully was born in Calcutta and worked for the BBC in South Asia for twenty-five years. He now works as a journalist in Delhi. He has written three books on India, including, most recently, *No Full Stops in India*.

Tom Owen Edmunds is one of the world's leading photographers. He has published two books of photographs, *Bhutan: Land of the Thunder Dragon* and *Mexico: Feast and Ferment*, as well as illustrating the book that accompanied the BBC series, *Great Journeys*.

Clive Anderson · *Natalia Makarova* · *Rian Malan*
Michael Palin · *Lisa St Aubin de Terán* · *Mark Tully*

GREAT RAILWAY JOURNEYS

With photographs by Tom Owen Edmunds

PENGUIN BOOKS
BBC BOOKS

PENGUIN BOOKS
BBC BOOKS

Published by the Penguin Group and BBC Worldwide Ltd
Penguin Books Ltd, 27 Wrights Lane, London w8 5tz, England
Penguin Books USA Inc., 375 Hudson Street, New York, New York 10014, USA
Penguin Books Australia Ltd, Ringwood, Victoria, Australia
Penguin Books Canada Ltd, 10 Alcorn Avenue, Toronto, Ontario, Canada m4v 3b2
Penguin Books (NZ) Ltd, 182–190 Wairau Road, Auckland 10, New Zealand

Penguin Books Ltd, Registered Offices: Harmondsworth, Middlesex, England

First published by BBC Books, a division of BBC Worldwide Ltd, 1994
Published in Penguin Books 1995
3 5 7 9 10 8 6 4

Maps by Line and Line

PICTURE CREDITS

1, 2 and 3 – Sajid Munir; 10 – Hugh Ballantyne; 14 – Stephen Pern
(Hutchison Picture Library); 27 – David Atchison-Jones.

All other photographs were taken by **Tom Owen Edmunds**

🅱🅱🅲 ™ BBC used under licence

Filmset by Datix International Limited, Bungay, Suffolk
Printed in England by Clays Ltd, St Ives plc
Set in 10.5/12.5 pt Bembo Monophoto

CONTENTS

KARACHI TO THE KHYBER

Mark Tully

Mark Tully's journey from Karachi to the Khyber

I often look lovingly at my 1910 *Bradshaw* and think of the days when trains really mattered in Britain. What makes Pakistan exciting is that they do still matter there. Neither cars nor aeroplanes have displaced them yet as the usual means of transport for a long journey. Almost anyone can travel, too – you don't have to have an expense account to afford a ticket. Stations are crowded, noisy places, where every arrival and departure is an occasion. The fact that the railways are still the mainstay of Pakistan's transport system gives passengers from countries meant to be more advanced the pleasurable impression that they have gone back in time. This impression is heightened by the stately progress trains make. Style has not been sacrificed for speed. Passengers can sit in the doorway, watching the cows come home in the evening and enjoying the unmistakable smell of village suppers cooking on dung fires.

Mind you, many Pakistanis don't appreciate their old-fashioned railway system. One of the officials I met when negotiating filming permission said: 'I only have one objection. To make a "positive" film about Pakistan Railways is a major disservice to the travelling public.' But then, making fun of the railways is just the survival of another tradition.

The Khyber Mail is, to me anyhow, the most romantic of all the trains which cross the subcontinent, yet in nearly twenty-five years living there I had never travelled on it. It runs the length of Pakistan, from Karachi near the mouth of the River Indus to

Peshawar at the foot of the Khyber Pass, a distance of 1050 miles. It takes two nights and a day to complete its journey, travelling at an average speed of about 32 miles per hour, which of course includes some lengthy stops at stations. The Mail often travels even slower than its schedule and is frequently subject to what railwaymen in Pakistan call 'late running', but then punctuality is no more the essence of a Pakistani railway journey than speed. If a train is scheduled to go fast you expect it to do just that, and get tense and irritated when it's even a few minutes late. In South Asia you happily hand over your destiny to the railways, and settle down to enjoy the luxury of being completely cut off from the rest of the world for the longer the better.

When I arrived at Karachi Cantonment, where the Khyber Mail starts, I was a little disappointed. I had expected something reminiscent of the military magnificence of Lahore Junction or the oriental Gothic exuberance of Bombay's Victoria Terminus. But Karachi Cantonment was a long, low, rather homely building, a station suited for a small, what used to be called 'up-country' town. Station Superintendent Syed Wasi Ahmed Rizvi, who greeted me on the steps of Karachi Cantonment, was proud of it. He was a small, Napoleonic figure dressed in an immaculate white uniform, who strutted proudly round his fiefdom barking orders to his underlings.

Within minutes Rizvi Sahib had our van unloaded and the cameras and film equipment safely stored in the VIP room. Every building of any importance in Pakistan has to have a room for Very Important Persons. The power that VIPs wield, their imperious demeanour and their erratic tempers, lead many officials to be obsequious to their so-called superiors, but I can't imagine the Station Superintendent of Karachi Cantonment falling at anyone's feet. He had just refused a promotion to Railway Headquarters in Lahore because, as he said to me, 'Here I am monarch of all I survey. In Railway Headquarters I would only rule over a peon [messenger]. I would be just another babu [clerk], not a railwayman.'

The Station Superintendent took me to the signal box high above the platforms, where he showed me how ancient and modern survive side by side on Pakistan Railways. There was a device for controlling the latest colour light signalling, but one of the signalmen was laboriously plotting the progress of trains by drawing lines on a chart with a pencil and ruler. The station announcer alternately broadcast the impending arrival of the Sind Express and read out prayers for the safe departure of the next train. When the British Raj ended in 1947, Pakistan was divided from India to fulfil the demand for a Muslim homeland. Islam is therefore the be-all and end-all of the nation.

The Khyber Mail was shunted into the platform well before its departure time. The mail had to be loaded into the travelling post office, where it would be sorted throughout the night and dropped off at the appropriate stations. The passengers' heavy baggage had to be booked into the luggage brake. The conductors had to deal with the inevitable arguments about reservations. Bribes had to be offered and sometimes taken – demand exceeds supply, and so there is a black market in berths.

While these preparations for the journey were being made, red-shirted coolies were pouring through the platform gates balancing loads of luggage on their heads. Chai-wallahs noisily urged passengers to have one more cup of tea before departure. The crowd on the platform grew denser and denser as more and more people came to see off their friends or relatives; it is a very lonely and sad Pakistani who can't find anyone to come and say goodbye at the start of a long railway journey. Above all the hubbub, the station announcer still vainly tried to make his voice heard.

To the uninitiated it looked like a scene of sheer chaos. I knew it was the anarchy of the subcontinent, out of which order of a sort always miraculously emerges. Sure enough, just before ten o'clock a shrill whistle rose above the din of departure, and the guard waved his green lamp. At the far end of the platform, the fireman put his head inside the cab and said to the driver, 'Right away.' There was a raucous blast from the diesel locomotive, and the Khyber Mail started slowly on its long journey. Passengers who were still saying their farewells scrambled aboard, forcing their way into crowded economy-class carriages. As I stood in splendid isolation in the open doorway of my first-class compartment, watching the platform pass and seeing the guard still waving his green light, I was reminded of my excitement as a child when the train which took us on family holidays used to pull out of Calcutta's Howrah Station. 'Diesel may have replaced steam,' I thought, 'but thank God little else has changed.'

As the train gathered speed I was shown to my compartment by the sleeping car attendant. It was what is known in the subcontinent as a coupé – a two-berth cabin, air-conditioned and with its own lavatory and washbasin. The attendant was inordinately pleased when I told him that in India even first-class air-conditioned passengers don't get their own loo. He asked whether Pakistan Railways were better than Indian in other ways, too; I said I would let him know when I finished my journey. Pakistanis seem to need constant reassurance that they are doing better than India, whether that's true or not. The ill will created by partition has led to a bitter rivalry between the two countries.

The Khyber Mail runs over the track of what was once the North Western Railway. It was the longest but by no means the most profitable of the railways of the Raj, starting from Delhi and going via Amritsar, the holy city of the Sikhs, to Lahore, the capital of Punjab. From Lahore one branch continued northwards to the military garrisons of Rawalpindi, Peshawar and the Khyber, while another went west to Karachi. At partition the whole system went to Pakistan except for the line from Delhi to Amritsar. The North Western was an amalgamation of several smaller companies which had developed in a somewhat haphazard fashion. The first engines to arrive at Lahore had to be sent by boat, and were hauled from the banks of the River Ravi by 102 bullocks and two elephants.

Although the railways have been perhaps the most lasting legacy of the British Raj, in 1844, when the first proposal to build a railway was put to the Directors of the East India Company, they were not convinced of its usefulness and suggested only limited experiments. Amongst the Directors' fears were 'the ravages of insects and vermin upon timber and earthwork'. A civil engineer thought that the surface of India was so uneven and overcrowded with cattle and goats that the lines would need to be suspended from chains at a height of at least eight feet above the ground. There were concerns about the commercial viability of the railways, too, although it's difficult to see how anyone could doubt they would overcome their main competition, the bullock cart. Then there were the potential passengers themselves, who were worried about making contact with people from other castes in crowded railway carriages, and wondered how they would find a train which started at an auspicious time. In the end commercial common sense, combined with defence needs, overcame all objections. Most of the North Western Railway consists of what were known as strategic lines – that is to say, lines where defence and not commerce was the reason for their construction.

On the first night of my journey I stayed up to watch the Khyber Mail cross the Indus and enter Hyderabad. That is Hyderabad Sind, not the perhaps better-known Hyderabad Deccan in South India, which was the seat of a Nizam equally renowned for his wealth and his parsimony. Our carriage was to be uncoupled at Hyderabad and shunted into the VIP siding so that we could be attached to a train which ran along the Indus valley in daylight.

Pakistan Railways had sent two senior officers with us to make sure that we got coupled to the right trains. One of them, Iqbal Samad Khan, was very senior indeed. He was the Chief Commercial Manager of Pakistan Railways – a thin man whose ever-present cigarette-holder clamped between his gapped teeth reminded me of the comedy actor Terry-Thomas. The other railway officer was Sardar Hussain Shah, Deputy Divisional Superintendent of Karachi. Shah was renowned for his unannounced nocturnal inspections. On one of them he surprised the wife of a signalman standing in for her husband. When Shah told her she could cause a serious accident she protested that she knew just as much about the job as her husband, so Shah tested her and found that to be perfectly true.

The railway officers were travelling in their own saloon made of teak, with a spacious sitting room, two bedrooms and a full-sized bath. Senior railway officers are entitled to attach one of these private saloons to certain trains, so that they can still travel in colonial style. Samad and Shah had arranged for a caterer with a full complement of cooks and bearers to travel with us and serve meals in the saloon.

After a very full English breakfast we were shunted on to the main line again and coupled to the Awam (People's) Express for the journey to the second bridge across the Indus. I made my way to the lower-class air-conditioned carriage, which does not have separate compartments but is like an open dormitory. At first the passengers were a little suspicious of me. They couldn't understand how a reporter who had covered so many dismal events in Pakistan's history, like the defeat of their army in 1971 when the Eastern Province of their country broke away to become Bangladesh, and the hanging of the former Prime Minister Zulfiqar Ali Bhutto in 1979, could be making an innocent film about a train journey. But passengers in Pakistan do not hide behind newspapers. For them it is impolite not to take an interest in their fellow passengers, and so I soon found myself drawn into conversation.

A ship's radio officer complained about the decline in shipping and the difficulty of getting work. He was on his way home and did not know when he would be recalled to Karachi. A business-man told me he had read my book *No Full Stops in India*, saying with a laugh, 'It was a pirated copy.' We went on to discuss my connection with his country and laughed again as he proposed I write another book, *No Punctuation Marks in Pakistan*. A retired civil servant, with the white beard and shaved upper lip of a pious Muslim, was on his way to see his new grandchild for the first time. The old man had been born and brought up in India, but had never been back since he left at partition. When I asked him why not, he said, 'This is my country now. We love it.' I couldn't but admire his patriotism, though I also felt saddened that he seemed to have no interest in a land that had been the home of his family for many generations. There must surely come a time when India and Pakistan will recover from the brutal surgery which divided them and start to restore the natural links between their two peoples.

Eventually the Awam Express pulled into Rohri, which is the junction for Quetta, the capital of Baluchistan. I had decided to make a diversion to Quetta because that line was one of the most challenging built by British engineers anywhere in the world.

As I got out of the carriage a photographer pushed through the crowd of coolies soliciting my business and started to click his camera ferociously. Wherever I went, whatever I did, he seemed to think it worthy of record. After some time I discovered that he was a boiler engineer who doubled as the official photographer for the Sukkur Division of Pakistan Railways.

An express from Lahore pulled up at the platform opposite, and out poured young men wearing green turbans loosely tied round their heads. They made a beeline for the taps where they washed their faces and their feet, chattering excitedly, before rolling out mats and kneeling to say their prayers. They were returning from a camp in Lahore where they had been trained for *tabligh* or propagating the faith, although in pious Pakistan I am not sure it needs much propagating. Passengers for Rohri itself streamed across the track in front of the train, ignoring the notices ordering them to use the footbridge and avoiding the ticket collectors at the gate.

I was to make the next stage of my journey on a permanent way inspector's trolley, two benches fixed back to back on a bogie of four wheels. Two men pushed the trolley until the engine spluttered into life, and we threaded our way through the points on to the Quetta branch. The trolley allowed me a good view of the first of the many engineering achievements of the Quetta line, the Lansdowne Bridge across the Indus.

When the Lansdowne's 820-foot-long (250 metres) span was slotted into place in 1889 it was the longest in the world, but it lost that record the next year to Scotland's Forth Bridge. The Lansdowne Bridge was first constructed in London and then dismantled and shipped out in pieces to be reassembled on the banks of the Indus. The men who designed and built it disparaged their colleagues who had to reassemble it, calling them 'mere Meccano engineers'. Later engineers have been full of praise for the ingenuity of those who erected the bridge – and somewhat critical of the designer. One wrote:

> It was almost as though the designer had gone out of his way to test the ability of the erector. Giant derricks, weighing 240 tons [243,852 kg] each and 230 feet [70 metres] long, made up of parts topping 5 tons [5080 kg] apiece, had to be erected leaning out over the water and at the same time inclining inwards in the plane at right-angles to the line of the bridge. And as if that was not difficult enough horizontal tie girders 123 feet [37.5 metres] long and weighing 86 tons [87,380 kg] each had to be put together 108 feet [33 metres] up in the sky.

This miracle of engineering aerobatics was completed with the loss of only six lives, and came in under budget too. There was a solemn ceremony to celebrate the opening of the bridge, the final link which at last allowed through running of trains from Lahore to Karachi. Instead of cutting the usual tape the Governor of Bombay unlocked a huge, ornate padlock, specially designed by Rudyard Kipling's father who was principal of the Art School in Lahore.

By the time I came to cross the Indus the Lansdowne Bridge had been relegated to carrying road traffic, and my trolley trundled across a bridge named after Pakistan's first military ruler, Field Marshal Ayub Khan. This aesthetically more pleasing bridge, suspended from a gigantic steel arch, ran alongside its predecessor. It did not suffer from the effects of high temperatures on a rigid steel structure, which had reduced the maximum running speed of trains crossing the Lansdowne Bridge to 5 miles per hour.

Two miles on from the bridge the inspection trolley drew into Sukkur Station. Sukkur is the headquarters of a railway division, and everyone from the Divisional Superintendent downwards was on the platform to greet us. Wherever we went, Pakistan Railways treated us like royalty. That evening there was a reception in our honour, and we were given an enormous dinner in the residential compound built for the railway officers. The compounds were provided to ensure a British way of life for the railway community and to keep them isolated from the 'native quarters'. It was all part of that determined effort made by the British to give the impression that they were a different and superior race. Pakistan Railway officers still live in splendid isolation from the dirt, dust, cacophony and chaos of a modern Pakistani town, but life has changed within the compounds. The change which affected me most that evening was prohibition.

On the way back from the reception to our air-conditioned carriage, parked once again in a VIP siding, we passed a cricket match being played in the middle of the road. Floodlit cricket may have caught on everywhere, but an appeal against bad light would certainly have been allowed in this case as play was illuminated only by street lamps. I often wonder how Pakistan produces such a fine international team when I see the conditions under which most Pakistanis play cricket.

The next stop was Jacobabad. I was a little apprehensive about this, because when I had first suggested spending the night there the senior railway official planning my journey had said, 'I wouldn't. Jacobabad has the largest mosquitoes in Pakistan.' But I decided it was worth braving the mosquitoes to visit the town named after General John Jacob, one of those legendary British officers who pacified the unruly provinces of Sind and Punjab in the mid-nineteenth century.

John Jacob left the tranquillity of his father's country vicarage to join the Bombay army at the age of sixteen, never to return to England. He was sent to a small frontier settlement on the edge of the desert which divided the plain of the Indus from the mountains that form the border with Afghanistan. There he raised his own regiments, ended the raids by tribesmen who used to come out of the mountains to loot and pillage the more fertile areas of Sind, and brought prosperity to the people. In his lifetime he planted a million trees, built over 300 miles of roads in an area where wheeled transport had been almost unknown, and brought the waters of the Indus to Jacobabad. During his time the population of the town rose from twenty-two civilians to ten thousand.

Jacob was a fiercely independent man who described the way he ruled the 120 miles of frontier under his control as 'common sense, hard labour, perseverance and watchfulness'. His relations with his superiors were not smooth. He once told the civilian administrator who was nominally his superior to 'leave much to [his] discretion and avoid all petty nonsense'. It's not surprising that he made many enemies among his fellow countrymen, but he was almost universally loved by the people he ruled. When he died in Jacobabad in 1858, just twelve years after assuming responsibility for what was then called Upper Sind, it is said that 'every man, woman and child in the place and for miles around came to see the procession, and the din and noise caused by the women tearing their hair and the men crying was indescribable'.

The love of John Jacob lives on, as I found when I went to his tomb where a large crowd had gathered to watch me pay my respects to him. The people told me they had refused to change the name of their town, although for reasons of national pride other places called after British officials now had new names. I was introduced to one of the town's sanitary inspectors, who in his spare time doubled as the guardian of the shrine of John Jacob. He told me that many men and women still came to the tomb to pray, especially if anyone in their family was suffering from fever. I couldn't claim to know of anyone suffering from fever, but I thought that a prayer at John Jacob's tomb might be an effective prophylactic against the legendary malarial mosquitoes of Jacobabad.

The sanitary inspector first lit sticks of incense and then scattered rose petals over the tomb. After that he told me to follow him as he walked round the tomb measuring it with red thread. Then he asked me whether I accepted that John Jacob was a *faqir* or miracle worker. When I said, 'I do,' he wound the thread which had measured the tomb into a necklace and put it round my neck. This remarkable ceremony was performed by a Muslim, using thread and incense which is usually associated with Hindu worship, honouring John Jacob, who was baptized a Christian and lived his life as an agnostic. I have learnt in the subcontinent to respect all religions, and so I vowed to wear the necklace until the thread rotted away. Six months later it was still there, and neither I nor anyone known to me had suffered from fever.

Being a forward-looking man, John Jacob had himself suggested that a railway should be built across the desert to the foot of the Bolan Pass which leads through the mountains to the Afghan border; but it took the Second Afghan War, more than twenty years later, to provide the spur. Once it did start, work proceeded at a remarkable pace – more than a mile of track was laid every day, through a desert of which the *Gazetteer of Sind* says 'the terror had for centuries been proverbial'. The line ended just below the mountains at Sibi, one of the many towns which competes for the title of the hottest place in the subcontinent. Nearby there is another town appropriately named Tanduri or 'oven-like'. So unpleasant is Sibi's reputation that there is a proverb which goes, 'Oh God, when thou hast created Sibi and Dudhar what point was there in creating hell?'

I was to travel across this fearsome desert to the hell-hole of Sibi on the footplate of a steam engine. One thing alarmed me a little: I learned that steam operating had long since been abandoned on this section, and there was now no facility to water an engine *en route*. I had visions of running dry in the middle of a desert in which, in 1915, thirty-two British soldiers had died of heat stroke while travelling in a train. Iqbal Samad, however, assured me that I had nothing to fear – that the two water tankers attached to our train would be more than enough to see us through the desert.

The train consisted of forty goods wagons, the railway officers' saloon, our first-class air-conditioned carriage, a dynamo car and those two water carriers. The engine standing at the head of this train in Jacobabad Junction had been built in Canada during the Second World War and was one of the last to be imported before Pakistan became independent. It had eight driving wheels and was designed for hauling goods trains. Because there was no steam working in the area any longer the engine had been towed all the way from Samasata, near Bahawalpur, more than 300 miles away, where in spite of its age it still used to run 150 miles every day.

To make sure that all went well on our journey across the desert the railways had sent Chowdhury Mohammad Shareef, a special foreman, from headquarters in Lahore. He was a white-haired perfectionist who seemed to know every rivet on a steam engine.

The new black paint of the engine shimmered in the sun. Its wheels and cow-catcher were painted silver. The railing round the boiler was covered with bright-coloured tinsel, and tinsel streamers were strung across the roof of the cab. The boiler and the firebox door were also lavishly decorated with brass plates. There was a crown on top of the funnel. The Pakistan flag flew from the front of the engine and there were models of Pakistani Airforce fighters above the two buffers. Inside the cab there was a picture of Mohammad Ali Jinnah, the founder of Pakistan, in one corner and Iqbal, the national poet, in the other. Everything possible had been done to demonstrate the crew's pride in their country and, of course, their engine. In Pakistan steam drivers still have their own locomotives.

Steam gushed out of the safety valve as we waited to start the run across the desert to Sibi. The driver, Nasir Ahmed, pulled a chain impatiently to give one short and one long blast on the whistle, indicating to the guard that he was ready to move off.

The guard, immaculately clad in a white quasi-military uniform, took a whistle out of his Sam Browne belt and blew long and loud; but the train did not move. The driver pulled the whistle cord again, this time two shorts and a long hoot. That was to tell the box to pull off the starter signal; but the arm of the signal remained obstinately at Stop. The fireman went to find out what was wrong and was told that traffic was jammed on the level crossing and the gates could not be closed. This took some time to sort out but eventually the signal arm fell, the driver opened the regulator, and we steamed slowly but surely out of the platform, the wheels screeching as we crossed the points on to the main line.

The engine slowly gathered speed and seemed all set for the desert, but then suddenly the driver saw two muddy black buffaloes mooching towards the track, impervious to all danger. He braked and the train lumbered to a halt, before the buffaloes got caught in the cow-catcher. Then we were off again.

The banging of the pistons, the rattling of the footplate, the hiss of steam and the roar of the fire all gave the impression of great energy and great speed, although in fact we probably never touched more than 40 miles per hour. Inside the cab the driver removed the wooden wedge to adjust the regulator, the fireman turned the red taps under the lubricators, and the inspector rapped the brass knob at the bottom of the water gauge to make sure all was well with the boiler.

We steamed into the desert, with sand blowing across the track. Fortunately it was early autumn and so the sun, though bright, was not unbearably hot. When the railway first crossed this desert it had no rival except camels. Now there is a road which runs parallel with the track for much of the way and is taking more and more of the traffic. Pakistan has made the same mistake as Britain — at least, I believe it's a mistake. It has invested in roads and ignored its railways. The railways still score on bulk transit for goods and on comfort and safety for passengers, but buses now do the journey from Karachi to Quetta in half the time the train takes and there are plans to build the country's first motorway. Unless the railways modernize, there must be a threat that passengers will desert the trains.

The line was single-track, and we were diverted into a loop at one small station in the middle of nowhere to wait for the mail from Quetta to pass. After two or three more stops, this time connected with our filming, the Locomotive Inspector began to get worried. We were well behind schedule and a sinister bubbling could be seen through the glass of the water gauge. The water in the gauge was becoming cloudy, too. The level in the boiler had to be reduced, otherwise the bubbles would get into the pistons. If that happened the bubbles would not condense like steam and so the pistons would break. A lower level in the boiler meant reduced speed. Reduced speed meant an even longer journey and greater risk of running out of water.

The sun was setting over the desert and the sky was salmon-pink when I first saw the mountains of Baluchistan in the distance. Dusk didn't last long; the darkness fell quickly. The tinsel streamers in the cab glittered in the light of an unshaded bulb. The headlight on the engine picked out the track as it ran through the dark desert.

When we were still some 40 miles from Sibi, the Inspector decided that he must stop to check the level in the two water tankers behind the tender. Mechanics and engineers appeared out of the darkness and started to discuss the crisis, but no one seemed able to calculate how much water we did have. Eventually one mechanic decided that the only answer was to take a look. He climbed on to the second tanker, dipped a rod inside it and announced that we could proceed with reasonable hope of reaching Sibi before we ran out of water.

The engine got under way again. The fireman threw sand through the hole in the door of the firebox. This apparently stopped the pipes getting blocked with carbon. He was always busy, even though he did not have the back-breaking job of shovelling coal as all Pakistan Railway steam engines burn furnace oil. Partition left the major coalfields in India, and Pakistan has always been reluctant to import anything from that country.

The fireman's next job was to turn a key in the floor to let a little more precious water into the boiler. He then took up position on the opposite side of the cab to the driver and stared ahead. I put my head out of the cab and saw the green oil light of a signal in the distance. Below it something seemed to be on fire. As we got nearer I saw that it was a flaming torch carried by a railwayman to let us know he was standing there with the token which would allow us to enter the next section of the line. The driver slowed down slightly and the fireman leaned out of the cab to hook his arm through the wire hoop holding the token.

After several more tokens had been exchanged, the driver announced that we were approaching the outer signal at Sibi. He gradually applied the brakes, and a journey which had lasted seven and a half hours ended. When I got down on to the platform my knees were knocking and I felt as unstable as a sailor who touches terra firma after a rough passage. It was as though I was still being shaken up by that wobbly, rattling footplate. But I was an intensely happy man. I had been on footplates before, but I had never made such an epic journey.

Sibi is the start of the line which runs through the Bolan Pass to Quetta and then on to the Afghan border. Four attempts were made to build a maintainable line to Quetta. Work on the first started in 1880, in the middle of the Second Afghan War, when the British feared the Tsar was planning to send his army through the Bolan Pass. The route chosen climbed nearly 6000 feet (1830 metres), through barren and almost uninhabited terrain. All the labourers and materials had to be brought from outside. Nine hundred camel-loads of food were consumed daily by the workers. The engineering hazards were enormous. The construction of one tunnel in the Nari Gorge cost so many lives that no worker would enter it unless he was paid five times the usual rate.

The railway also had to pass through a long, narrow, dark gorge called the Chappar Rift, whose cliffs rose hundreds of feet straight up from the bed of a stream which frequently turned into a raging torrent. The line had to travel well above the river bed, but the rocks were too unstable to allow a ledge to be cut in the side of the cliff. The engineers therefore decided that the only answer was tunnels – in total length more than one mile. It was hard enough to get labourers to the remote gorge because of the floods which frequently blocked its narrow entrances, but it was harder still to get them into positions where they could start work. The problem was overcome with that ingenuity which characterized the work of Victorian engineers. Labourers were lowered from the clifftop on platforms, and then had to gain their own foothold on the sheer rockface to start blasting with gunpowder.

All that work in the Chappar Rift came to naught just fifty-five years after the line was opened. A particularly severe flood washed away the track outside tunnel number thirteen, even though it was some 200 feet (61 metres) above the river bed. By then an alternative route to Quetta had been built, there were only two trains on the Chappar route, and many more important lines on the North Western had been breached by the floods. So, sadly but not entirely unjustifiably, it was decided to abandon the line.

Having heard such evil reports about Sibi, I decided to waste no time there and the next morning to start my journey up the Quetta line which had survived. I was allowed to sit in the cab of the diesel pulling the Quetta Express. We were soon roaring across the desert, driving straight for a wall of yellow mountains. Just when a head-on collision seemed unavoidable, a narrow crack in the mountainside opened up. We shot through it, lurched round a corner and were inside a tunnel before I had time to draw breath. We were hardly aware of the bright sunlight before we were back in the darkness of another tunnel. Tunnel after tunnel eventually took the train into the broader valley of a dried-up river. The only vegetation was a sort of cactus whose prickles camels somehow digest. Then we came to more tunnels. The shale looked unstable enough to tumble over the portals of the tunnels at any moment. We crossed and recrossed the dried-up river bed. It had taken engineers three attempts to build a line which could survive the monsoon, when water poured down that river bed carrying all in front of it.

We passed a small camel caravan, the first of the nomads making their way from the highlands of Baluchistan to winter in the plains of Sind with their sheep, goats and dogs. The train snaked its way up the valley until we reached the station of Abi-Gum, where the engine known as the banker was coupled to the back of the train to give us a push because the gradient was getting steeper. From there it was a short climb to Mach with its yellow-walled jail, reputed to be one of the least pleasant places in Pakistan.

In more leisurely days Mach was the station where passengers used to get out for a meal and change from the clothes they had been wearing in the heat of the plains to something more suited to the colder mountain climate. It's also the main railway town between Sibi and Quetta, with its own engine shed where the bankers are housed. Another banker was added to our train for the really ferocious climb ahead. To get a good start at the gradient engines take off very suddenly from Mach, and passengers are warned that they will miss the train if they try to jump aboard at the last moment.

At Hirok the line rose like a switchback, but the driver opened the throttle and we charged ahead without any apparent difficulty. The driver told me that it had required much more skill and hard work to get a steam engine up this gradient. He said, 'In those days we were fit because we really had to work. Now our tummies are coming out.'

We stopped again at Kolpur, which is the summit of the pass. An abandoned watchtower, a remainder of the days when tribal people used to raid the railways, looked down from the mountains on the small station below. At the end of Kolpur Station we passed through yet another tunnel and started our descent to the plain of Quetta, a great bowl surrounded by high mountains. Here there was some sign of cultivation. Camels ploughed fields, and the drab grey of the valley was broken by small patches of green orchards. We passed Spezand, the junction for the line which goes all the way to the Iranian border, a line that is only used by two passenger trains a week each way.

As we reached the outskirts of Quetta itself the driver put his hand on the horn and the train roared through the houses and bazaars lining the track. The young men and the old, women and children perched on the track flew up like hens disturbed on their roost.

At Quetta Station itself there was an unpleasant surprise awaiting me. Grey-uniformed police came on board the train and ordered me not to get out because there was a demonstration against me. The BBC's Urdu Service has a vast audience in Pakistan. This makes both politicians and officials particularly sensitive to what the Urdu Service reports, and there have been several controversies as a result, but I couldn't imagine how anyone could object to our railway journey. I was particularly upset because I knew that a demonstration in Quetta would spark off trouble everywhere else we went and might even mean abandoning the film. But I needn't have worried. Iqbal Samad soon found out that the police had got it all wrong – the demonstration was against the government's Kashmir policy.

That wasn't the only thing the Quetta police got wrong. A few days later we were filming a train entering Quetta Station when a posse of policemen pounced on us like a pack of wild dogs. They wouldn't listen to our government liaison officer, they wouldn't read our official permission, but dragged us into a van and drove to the nearest police station. There our government liaison officer told the burly Baluch inspector in no uncertain terms that he had been insulted.

The inspector called for the sergeant who had arrested us and shouted at him, 'Can't you read? Are you blind? Can't you recognize a government official when you see one?'

The head constable stammered, 'But sir, but sir, the tall Angrez swore at us in filthy Urdu.'

The inspector didn't bother to find out whether I had sworn at his head constable or not; he knew that was one of the standard excuses for a wrongful arrest. He told the sergeant he would deal with him later, apologized profusely to our liaison officer and said we could continue filming. That was all very well, but we had missed the train we wanted to film. Our liaison officer said the next train was the Chilton Express – but, he warned, 'It doesn't have any time.'

'What do you mean?' I asked.

'Nobody ever knows what time it will come in. It travels through parts of Punjab where the local landlords, not the station-master, decide when the train should leave.'

So we decided we could do without that shot.

Quetta is 6000 feet (1830 metres) above sea level. It's a small, dusty town dominated by the intrigues of Baluch and Pathan tribal leaders. When the British eventually took control of the place they made it the headquarters of the army guarding that section of the Afghan frontier from Russian invasion, and set up the Indian Army Staff College there.

The Pakistan Army has preserved its British traditions even more lovingly than the Railway has. The Staff College Museum contains the room where a certain Colonel B. L. Montgomery lived when he was an instructor. His desk, his chair, his clock and his small black oil stove are still there. The museum also houses the military regalia of the first officer to command the college, Major General Sir A. W. L. Bayley, including his black plumed hat. There is a picture of General Kitchener, who commanded the whole of the Indian Army, and a Royalty Room – the royalty commemorated being British.

In the great hall of the Staff College Mess, surrounded by silver military trophies, I met General Ali, the present comman-dant. A tall, handsome man dressed in an immaculately cut suit, he told me with pride that his own regiment had been raised by General Jacob and that he was the third generation to serve in it. Although he was very much a Pakistani, he believed that the Army should still be proud of its British traditions too. When it was first suggested that men like General Ali's grandfather should be offered commissions, many officers protested that they would never come up to the standards of British public-school boys. The irony is that the one place you are likely to find those standards upheld now is in a Pakistan Army mess.

I didn't have time to travel back to the main line by train, so with considerable misgivings I decided to fly to Lahore. Before catching the train for the next stage of my journey I went to see the General Manager of the Railways. The headquarters are in the same red-brick building which housed the senior officers of the North Western Railways. The administrative practices of a late Victorian railway still flourish in its rabbit warren of offices. The corridors are thronged with peons or messengers carrying files tied up with faded pink tape, bearers with trays of tea, and babus or clerks gossiping for lack of anything better to do. In the office of the General Branch I approached a man sitting behind a notice which read 'Pivot General'. Apparently this was the centre around which the files of the railway headquarters rotated, in a never-ending circle of buck passing. The Pivot General ordered a messenger, 'Take him to GM sahib's office.'

The General Manager, Zahoor Ahmad, sat behind a large desk with pictures of the men who had sat at the same desk, from Colonel Wallace in 1887 onwards, looking down on him. In one corner stood a clock which had been made for the Scinde Railway before it was amalgamated into the North Western. The clock, needless to say, still kept immaculate time. The General Manager did admit that past Pakistan governments had not given the railways the priority they deserved, but he was confident that this one would step up investment. He was remarkably bullish about the future of his antiquated system, saying that goods and passenger demand still far exceeded supply. When I raised the question of the dreaded motorway the General Manager said he wasn't bothered. He believed that he could buck the trend elsewhere in the world and hold out against the road threat.

Fine colonial buildings like the high court, the museum and indeed the railway headquarters, together with broad, tree-lined avenues, parks and canals, all give the not entirely unfair impression that Lahore is the best preserved of all the cities of the Raj. But there was a Lahore before the British came, and it still survives in the Moghul monuments and the bazaars surrounding them.

I had a little time before my next train left and so I decided to take a ride through one of the bazaars in a tonga or pony trap, still an efficient form of transport in those narrow lanes. Tongas have been displaced in India by cycle-rickshaws, but Pakistan takes pride in the fact that it does not use humans to pull vehicles.

As the well-fed pony clip-clopped through the bazaar the driver told me that he wanted the British back, because life was much less expensive in their days. I don't know how he could possibly have got the impression that modern Britain could manage anyone's economy; perhaps he just said that because he thought I would like to hear it. I stopped to drink sweet tea with a group of musicians who were complaining that the mullahs' dislike of music was affecting their business. I watched harmoniums being made by hand, and leather thongs being tied round drums. I saw a political pamphlet being printed on a small press. I drank lassi, a yoghurt shake, and discussed politics, a neverending source of conversation in the subcontinent. Then my tonga turned towards the railway station.

Lahore Station, like so many in the turbulent territory that the North Western Railway ran through, was built like a fort. When I congratulated the Superintendent, Mohammed Afzal, on his magnificent station he said, 'You built it. We haven't added a single brick since independence.' Then he went on with a smile, 'Of course, we may have taken one or two away.' He told me my train to Rawalpindi was a little late because the electric locomotive had broken down a few miles outside the station. Only about 175 miles of the main line have been electrified, and this means that most passengers are unaccustomed to the dangers of overhead wires. The railway timetable politely 'requests passengers in their own interests not to travel on footboards of trains; not to travel on the roofs of the carriages;

and not to lean out of doors and windows of carriages' when trains are travelling on the electrified sector. According to the Station Superintendent, remarkably few do. He said only about one person a year got electrocuted by travelling on the roof.

The six-hour journey to Rawalpindi was eventful. We crushed a scooter at a level crossing. Fortunately the owner had run for it when he realized he couldn't get across before the train. Our next unscheduled halt was due to mechanical trouble. Because of shortage of foreign exchange the railways had over the years been forced to beg for engines from various aid donors. This had led to the acquisition of what Iqbal Samad described as a 'zoo of locomotives', each species having different spare parts, with all the difficulties that causes. Fortunately spare parts were no problem this time – a brick for a hammer and some string were all that the driver needed – and we were soon on our way.

Walking down the train, I came across a confrontation between a ticket inspector and a ticketless traveller. The traveller paid up very reluctantly, saying that if we hadn't been filming the incident he would have got off with a small bribe. Then there was another halt, because someone had pulled the communication cord so that he could get off the train near his own home. The fine for that crime is still the same as it was under the British, and there is very little risk of being caught anyhow.

We reached Pindi after dark, to be greeted by one of my favourite people in the whole of the subcontinent – Mohammad Salim, taxi driver. The first thing he told me was that his wife had given birth to yet another child – her eighth, if I remember rightly. I have driven with Salim for fifteen years, and we have seen many good and some bad times together. When the military dictator General Zia ul-Haq was annoyed with my coverage he took it out on Salim by arresting him. I attempted to intervene with the Superintendent of Police, but that night some of Salim's friends came to my room and said, 'Don't interfere. Salim has been beaten up again just because you complained about his arrest.'

The next day Salim drove me to the Garrison Church for

Sung Eucharist. There were brass plaques on the walls commemorating the lives of those who had died to bring a Christian civilization to India. Many, like Lieutenant A. R. Murray, had died very young. He survived the Second Afghan War, only to be brought down by cholera at the age of twenty-four. I couldn't claim to be a good Christian, but I love the Church. In fact my first choice of career was the Anglican Ministry, but the Bishop of Lincoln quite rightly realized I was not suited to the Church. (My second choice, incidentally, was the railways, but British Rail rejected me too.) Being somewhat sentimental, tears came to my eyes as we sang one of my favourite hymns very slowly in Urdu.

The celebrant was the Bishop of Lahore, a courageous man who has fought many battles for the small community which is the legacy of all that Christian endeavour. He was currently leading a movement against the government's plans to include religion on identity cards. He feared that this was the first step towards declaring that only Muslims could be full citizens of Pakistan.

Pindi to Peshawar is the last stage of the Khyber Mail's journey. By this time many of the carriages have been shed, partly because there is not that much traffic on the sector, and partly because the loop lines where crossings take place are too short to take a full-length train. Speeds between Rawalpindi and Peshawar are slower, too. It takes the Khyber Mail four hours and five minutes to cover 108 miles – an average speed of just 27 miles per hour. That is partly because, although it's meant to be a long-distance train linking the main cities of Pakistan, the Khyber Mail stops at an inordinate number of small stations in the early hours of the morning as it completes the last stage of its run to Peshawar.

I had decided not to take the Khyber Mail, which ran overnight on this section, but to complete my journey to Peshawar by day, stopping off at various places *en route*. My first halt was at Golra Sharif. It's a small junction called after a local Muslim saint whose shrine is in the village.

The parrots were squawking in the *paakar* and *peepal* trees which had stood on the platform since the railway was built. The walls of the station were being whitewashed; the station-master denied that this was because we were going to film there. He said whitewashing was done regularly to remove the dried droppings of the swallows which nest in the station, and cannot be driven away because they are sacred. Business is apparently falling off at Golra Sharif, and a number of trains have been taken out of the timetable.

From Golra Sharif the line makes its way through rocky, undulating countryside, with mountains in the distance, until it comes to a point high above the Indus where the Attock Bridge crosses the river. In 1926 it was decided that the bridge should be reconstructed – and a good thing too, because during the work it was discovered that one of the supports was standing on a rock which was crumbling like a decayed tooth. I got down here to watch the train cross the bridge. It's a double-decker, but the road below the railway has now been replaced by a new bridge, and there were only some villagers driving their goats home as the train rumbled overhead.

Beyond the bridge the line runs along the gorge for a short distance but turns away before the blue waters of the Indus meet the muddy brown Kabul River. There is only one more impor-tant station before Peshawar, Nowshera. With its schools of armour and artillery, it's one of the most important centres of the Pakistan Army. Some 30 miles further on, the outskirts of Peshawar start. It's a city which has expanded because of refugees from Afghanistan. The leaders of the Mujahiddin made it their headquarters during the war which showed that the weaponry of a modern superpower was no match for the Afghans' courage and their skill in guerrilla warfare, passed down from generation to generation. Afghans pride themselves on never having been defeated.

In Peshawar there was no room at the old-fashioned Deans Hotel, so I had to stay at the modern Pearl Continental. There was a notice by the reception desk saying: 'Arms cannot be brought inside the hotel premises. Personal guards or gunmen are requested to deposit their weapons with the hotel security. We seek your cooperation – The Management.' I am sure the management does not always get that cooperation, because every man in the North West Frontier Province regards it as his right to carry a gun.

Preferring Pathan cooking to the Pearl Continental's, I went out that evening to the Medina mosque which is surrounded by small restaurants, with carcasses of goats hanging from butchers' hooks outside. The proprietors sit cross-legged, cutting meat with knives held between their toes. Their speciality is goat cooked in a *karhai*, which is somewhat similar to a Chinese wok. Tomatoes, chillies and *dhaniya* or coriander are added, and the meat is then cooked, I was told, 'until it speaks'. If it's a little tough, some water is added. My *karhai gosht* was beautifully tender, and I managed not to be put off my food by the basket under my table full of bones discarded by earlier diners.

Peshawar should have been the end of my journey, because the line which runs on to the summit of the Khyber was officially closed during the Soviet–Afghan war – although one Englishman who lived in Peshawar in those days did tell me he had seen some ammunition trains being hauled up the pass. By great good fortune, however, Pakistan Railways had just decided to revive the line for tourists and they put on a preliminary train for our film.

Two steam engines, once again resplendent in their black livery and magnificently adorned, awaited me just the other side of Peshawar Airport. It was a push-me-pull-you train, with the engine at the front pointing towards the Khyber and the engine at the other end pointing back towards Peshawar. I was told that the engines had been built in 1913 and 1919 in Britain, but were still quite capable of making the long haul up the Khyber. The train consisted of a restaurant car, a parlour car, a generator and a brake van. We were the only passengers, but there was an army of railway employees to accompany us.

I climbed on to the footplate of the front engine and we

27

edged slowly forward on a flat stretch of line running through the suburbs of Peshawar. I felt inordinately proud as we moved majestically through the crowds which had turned out to see the Khyber train running again. At a level crossing terrified tonga ponies reared in their shafts, shivering with fear, nostrils flaring; they had never seen snorting monsters like the steam engines which were bearing down on them.

We were soon in sight of the narrow V in the rampart of mountains ahead which marked the entrance of the Khyber. The inspector who had travelled with me from Jacobabad to Sibi was on the footplate again. He rechecked all the gauges and had a hurried word with the driver to make sure we were fully prepared for the long climb. Then we lumbered through the entrance to the Khyber and were engulfed by the pass. The beat of the pistons grew longer and longer and echoed off the barren yellow mountains. Mechanics sat on the front of the engine waiting to pounce on any fault which might develop. I looked back as we rounded yet another corner and saw the Pakistan flags fluttering proudly below the boiler of the back engine. The smoke from its funnel left a dark patch in the bright, clear, sunlit air. Then we plunged into one of the thirty-four tunnels. Smoke filled my eyes and the roar of not one but two engines deafened me. I could well imagine how the Amir of Afghanistan, a land without trains, got so alarmed when passing through the longest tunnel on the North Western that he pulled the communication cord.

Eventually we ground to a halt at the first of the zigzags, where the gradient is so steep that the train has to reverse to climb it. Pathan tribesmen, all armed, appeared from nowhere to watch the train change direction, and the rear engine become the front one. Above us we could see the second zigzag, where the original order would be restored. We had some difficulty in getting away from the second change of direction: there were anxious consultations on the telephone connected to the engine at the back. It was essential that the rear engine should get the train moving before we opened our regulator, otherwise we would pull the train apart. After much huffing and hooting I felt the train move forward slightly, our driver let steam into the cylinders and we resumed our slow but steady progress until we reached the grim, high-walled Shagai fort. There we stopped to take water.

From Shagai the line levelled out a little and the yellow shale gave way to blue limestone. We passed some of the small fortresses in which Pathan families live – enclosures surrounded by high, windowless walls built of baked mud. Then we came to a school, where the children poured out to greet us. Some just stared wide-eyed in amazement; it's possible they had never seen a train before. Some jumped up and down and clapped excitedly. Some, the more audacious, stood on the line, daring each other to be the last to get off.

Even the innovative engineers who had built the Bolan line considered the Khyber to be impassable by rail, but after the Third Afghan War in 1919 it was decided that an effort would have to be made. British troops were now posted at the summit of the Khyber, and they needed a railway to supply them. One of the first jobs was to persuade the Pathan tribal leaders to accept a railway running through their territory. They were totally opposed to it until Victor Bayley, the engineer who was to build the railway, told them that the trains would be very slow and therefore easy to loot. After that the Pathans even agreed to be the contractors.

It was dangerous terrain to work in, and the support of the tribal leaders was always uncertain. The British political agent warned Bayley, 'Whether it's the climate or the underlying strain under which we all live, a man cracks up suddenly if he goes on too long. It's no place for weaklings.' An army officer told him to be very careful of the Pathans, saying, 'They are pretty poisonous blighters.' Bayley himself found them 'murderous ruffians', but then went on to say that they were not much different from contractors anywhere else in the world.

The conditions under which Bayley had to work were not easy, either. Much of the material had to be carried up the mountainside by donkeys so hardy that when a lorry ran into a pack of them they all survived. In high winds the surveyors' theodolites blew over, and in the extreme heat a haze made the sightings waver. But Bayley persevered, and after five years trains ran to the Afghan border – making India, in his view, 'impregnable for the cost of a single battleship'.

Our train steamed slowly into Landi Kotal, the summit of the Khyber and the end of the line. The track which ran from there down the mountains to the Afghan border below had been taken up before the British left. The entire population of the small town, renowned for its smugglers and its handicraft – arms manufacturing – seemed to be on the platform. The station itself is a two-storeyed fort built of stone and surrounded by a high wall, behind which the staff live. The only access to the public is a small booking office window which can double as a machine-gun loop.

I was taken through the grim gates in the high wall to the courtyard to meet the staff and have my last cup of tea with Pakistan Railways. Then I went to say farewell to the train. The two engines stood against the background of the brown mountains. Smoke curled from their funnels as they rested from their great labour. Their green Pakistan flags fluttered proudly. It was evening. Hauling tourists is far less gallant than holding the Khyber Pass, but only holidaymakers can now prevent night falling over that unique railway and its proud engines.

Landi Kotal has become a Pakistan Army garrison, but the cap badges of the British regiments who served there are still emblazoned on the mountainside. Among them are the Dorsets, with their honour '*Primus in Indis*', awarded to them because they were the first king's regiment – as opposed to the regiments of the East India Company – to serve in the subcontinent. The Dorsets, the Gordon Highlanders, the South Wales Borderers, the York and Lancasters, the 22nd of Foot the Cheshires and the other British regiments which were stationed at Landi Kotal have long gone but their traditions live on in the Khyber Rifles, who mounted a special parade for us complete with a pipe band.

The traditions of the Pathans live on, too. The Pakistan government still treats them with special care. The penal code does not operate in their territory: justice is administered not by courts but by *jirgahs* or tribal assemblies. But the tribal system is gradually crumbling. Roads have now opened up the terrain and the Pathans are doing very well in transport and other businesses. This is introducing alien concepts into their ancient way of life. I fear that the railways will have to modernize, too. If they don't, the strategic lines to the Afghan border, surely among the greatest monuments of the railway age, will fall prey to some Pakistani Dr Beeching. I just hope that modernization does have a human face, and that the Khyber Mail does not become just the ten o'clock intercity to Peshawar.

SANTOS TO SANTA CRUZ

Lisa St Aubin de Terán

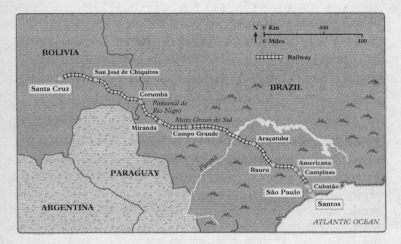

Lisa St Aubin de Terán's journey from Santos to Santa Cruz

I have set out to travel from the Atlantic Ocean to the foothills of the Bolivian Altiplano, from the once famous coffee town of Santos to the newly famous drug city of Santa Cruz de la Sierra. I have made other great railway journeys by chance, but never by design; this is to be a 'proper journey' with a beginning and a prearranged destination. The pace will be dictated less by my caprice than by the vagaries of the Brazilian Railways. It is early March and I have left the sharp frosts of a late Italian winter for the steamy heat of the tail-end of a tropical rainy season.

Santos is a fading city spilling into the sea with a constant flow of debris and reminders of past splendour. The coffee that was once Brazil's greatest wealth has been virtually squeezed off the international market by foreign competition and a boom in local orange juice. Some of the nineteenth-century villas of the coffee merchants are now only hollow masks propping each other up. The old port is still the largest in Latin America, but the style of the place has lost its balance and the grandeur has gone, leaving only the hordes of sailors and prostitutes. However, it is saved from seeming a sad place (being so polluted and riddled with disease) by its beach life and the reverence with which it is held in the hearts of Brazilians. Forget the coffee and the past, Santos is where Pele comes from: the king of football was born here. Beyond the heat haze and the pounding rhythm of transistor radios on the beach, and beyond the sinister lines of grey cargo ships on the horizon, and beyond the immediate relief of street vendors on the promenade shuffling reluctantly in and out of their day-long siestas to sell their green coconuts, ice cream and fried fish, there is a halo: Pele's. His fame is the achieved dream of every Brazilian boy and the pride of his nation. Pele has, by association, lifted his home town way above the litter and the rubble and the piles of used syringes and the unsavoury sea that washes over its shore.

The initial impact on arriving in Santos is the glare, then the heat and the tide of half-naked people surging towards the water. I have never seen so many well-gestated paunches bulging out of so many mini nylon trunks, nor so many tanga-traumatized buttocks. As I drink from my first green coconut, having tried out my very rusty Portuguese to get it, the vendor follows my glance towards the jogging flesh. 'The best ones go to Rio,' he says with a shrug. He steps delicately over a bright green lizard, slumps back into his plastic director's chair and drifts back into the half-sleep I had roused him from. In Santos there are pyramids of green coconuts and battered tin trolleys full of them, tended by various somnambulants with languorously smiling eyes, appalling dentistry and mutating skin afflictions.

Every few minutes, people come up and ask me my name and if I like Santos. Between assuring strangers how fond I am of their city, I think about it and decide that I really am. I like the sight of so many people enjoying the sun and the sand and their celebration of themselves. I like the blend of drowsiness and spontaneous prattle that gives a marionette-like quality to the promenade.

I have bought a guide book and map of Brazil which I study in the same sporadic way as my neighbours study each other's flesh. I am lulled by the general feeling of well-being, of drifting with the tide. I have never had any sense of direction, which is, perhaps, why I feel so safe on a train. Trains move implacably along their own tracks, pausing only at predestined places.

I feel at home in Brazil; I can even evoke my paternal grandfather, a moustachioed Señor Mendonça from Belem, to put me further at my ease. Bloated as I am with coconut water and roasting under 100°F (38°C), the sensual hum of warring radio stations is lulling me to sleep. I have a train to catch, though. I ask the time and a series of Chinese whispers goes in search of a watch.

The station at Santos was opened in 1867 and is now part of the state-owned Federal Railway network (RFFSA). It too is like a hollow façade; there is little beyond its ornate exterior except a sense of space and a queue jostling to funnel past a ticket man in a glass booth. Most of the passengers are day trippers from São Paulo. The empty interior is decorated with blue and white tiles like a Brazilian church, and like the Church it offers the promise of another life.

As soon as the dilapidated, peeling, silver train leaves Santos, it begins to climb through the rich verdure which is the legacy of the rainy season. The sky is alive with magpies. Wherever the ground is highest, small villages huddle back to back and belly to belly, jutting out on their outcrops with a narrow hem of gardens full of washed-out hydrangeas, spindly papaya trees and washing lines trickling into the swallowing undergrowth. Lilies grow wild by the hundreds, filling the air with their heady fragrance.

The São Paulo train then passes through some of the most stunningly beautiful vegetation I have ever seen. This is one of the last pockets of the Atlantic rainforest, 95 per cent of which has been destroyed. Here the lilies have multiplied to hundreds of thousands and cover every available expanse along the tracks and under the trees, merging with scarlet montbretia, clumps of ferns and the ubiquitous blue morning glory. The scent is of the lilies and the damp humus, but the predominant sight is of the quaresmeira tree which takes its name from Lent, at which time every year it blooms with startling purple and white flowers. The rainforest presents a uniform ceiling of dozens of tropical and subtropical trees; anything growing over that height becomes smothered by lichen and strangled by orchids. Thus, apart from the occasional palm tree, the only trunks to pierce the high mottled ceiling die from the top down and stand out in skeletal pallor, victims of the tall poppy syndrome, reduced to being perches for hawks and vultures and whitewashed with their guano.

Cut through the vegetation there are vast, stone-lined gullies, built by the British to drain away the torrential rains from the rails. It is hard to steal a moment from the scenery to pay homage to the daring engineering, the vision and the sacrifices required to build this line. I begin to be governed by hearsay, stopping off at places that have been recommended to me along the line. This is an anglophile stretch, all built by the British, who have left a trail of memorabilia behind them. In 1848, they built a winding gear to haul trains up the steep incline from Santos to Paranapiacaba, which means the place from which you can see the sea – as I am assured one can before eleven o'clock in the morning. After that, it is swallowed by a mist so dense that the station buildings seem to hover over the edge of the world; to venture beyond is an act of faith. The railways brought work, mobility, stability, the first cinema, football and a simplified version of cricket, so anything to do with trains is regarded with affection. Children in bright T-shirts and cotton shorts stand by to wave as the train arrives.

Paranapiacaba shrouded in mist has a moody, mysterious feel like being in a time warp: its meticulously-built brick hangars are immense and surreal. In one, a collection of antique carriages is preserved. There is the Emperor Pedro II's private compartment crowned with blue glass (glass, shutters, tombstones, houses, lorries and even weeds seem to be blue here in Brazil). There is a British locomotive from 1907 and a funeral car from the same year, with a place for the coffin at one end and rows of wicker chairs for the mourners at the other. The cheerful directions of a group of railway workers gave no indication of this ghostly desolation. I feel like a grave-robber violating a tomb. I grew up next to the Transport Museum in London, paying court to state carriages and famous engines that were all cordoned off from the public and out of bounds. These ones are open to the corrosive touch of mist and men alike, but the voracious local midges are a plague and they prevent me from prying any longer.

I return, via the tracks, stepping over the slippery, eroded hardwood sleepers. I ask when the next train to São Paulo arrives and am greeted by toothless amusement. This is still the first stretch of my projected two thousand or so miles, and it is one of the shortest legs, so I find it slightly unnerving that all attempts to establish a timetable are met with either diametrically contrasting answers or hilarity. I find I have so much time that I may as well be a moving target to the midges, and return to the railway remains to see the hauling gear which is the pride of Paranapiacaba. To get there entails crossing the equivalent of the paupers' cemetery, past burnt out and abandoned trains rusting into their tracks.

Then a train whistles into the station, apparently unexpectedly, and I have a job to catch it. This seems to be a day for mood swings. After the place from where you could see the sea were it not for the fog, I become lost again in a trance of banana palms, entangling morning glory, lilies and yellow butterflies when, without any warning, Cubatão looms into view. It is an industrial nightmare, a suppurating sore grafted on to the edge of the rainforest, spewing out chemical waste through its massive, glinting factory chimneys. The train stops at Cubatão, and then seems incapable of continuing until it recovers from the ecological shock. There is a barrel of tar burning on the platform together with a token pile of rubbish. The station-master is deep in conclave with his men in a small, noisy room that he appears both to work from and to live in. I stand on the platform contemplating the town above me, the brutality of its position and its capacity for pollution. A convoy of buses progresses along a flyover beyond the station. There are dozens of them, busing the factory workers home, crawling along the horizon like determined insects inching into a desperate future. My reverie is interrupted by a piercing whistle; straggling passengers move off the tracks, and the train snakes on to São Paulo.

Cubatão was the trailer, but São Paulo is the B-movie, the

heartland of ugliness. When in the sixteenth century the party of Jesuit priests led by Nóbrega and de Anchieta founded São Paulo on the high Piratinanga plateau, they could not have had so much as an inkling of the urban chaos they were unleashing.

The ride from the station, Estação da Luz, to my hotel feels like circling round the suburbs of hell, through an oppressively grey, concrete tunnel towering and squatting in an unkempt maze. São Paulo is a stretcher of negative expectations; every time I think I have seen the most depressing, unattractive street possible, yet another proves itself to be worse and even drabber. Nearly twenty million people are packed into this urban labour camp, of whom one and a half million live in *favelas* (shanties) and six hundred thousand live on the streets.

Breakfast is a tropical banquet, a self-service meander around plates of papaya, melon, watermelon, pineapples, dozens of breads and cakes and exotic cocktails. I find myself sharing a queue with a Japanese football team and their manager. They have come from Japan to play Corinthians, the famous São Paulo team founded by British railway workers. It is to be a friendly match with only a small crowd, and I am invited along. I am not usually a football fan, but I feel quite maudlin about Pele, so I go.

I sit on a cream concrete terrace under a punishing sun with a handful of adoring fans. Corinthians have two national players in their team today, while the Japanese have fans from São Paulo's large Japanese enclave. Horns and Japanese whistles are sounded off to chants, but the atmosphere is relaxed. No one actually falls asleep, but there is a sense of siesta cum fiesta which is a pleasant relief from the city's grey slums.

São Paulo is a disturbing place, unsettling and unsettled and profoundly depressing; to spend more than a few hours there is to become the public prosecutor, amassing fat dossiers of damning statistics and incriminating evidence. The city produces 11,000 tons of rubbish per day, the Federal Police murder four street children per week, a thousand families live under the viaduct, one of the largest *favelas* is built directly over the city's water supply. Much of the air pollution is self-inflicted – raised dust from the red-dirt roads. There are six hundred thousand child prostitutes in Brazil, many of them dragged from the streets of São Paulo.

The early morning of my third day here finds me in the Praça da Sé on the steps of the cathedral, waiting for a Jesuit priest, Padre Lancelotte, who works with the street people. Even the cathedral is grey and ugly and built in 1954. There are fresh bloodstains on its steps, and a gaggle of eight-year-olds alternately picking at a box of popcorn and sniffing scarlet shoemakers' glue. The box of popcorn is communal; the clear plastic glue bags are not. Entire families begin to crawl out from under the cement pools of an elaborate system of civic fountains: there is a gap of a few feet between the cement and the ground which has become home to hundreds of vagrant Paulistanos. Others doss on benches and under them, against kerbs, in doorways, outside shops – anywhere they can. These *gente do rúa*, or *miserables*, gather in the Praça da Sé because there are hot air vents from the metro there, and there used to be a market. This is a city of waste, and the poor live on leftovers. The Ministry of Justice in the Praça da Sé is, appropriately, draped in black for its restoration.

Despite the crack on the streets, and the violence, the hordes of one-legged beggars and the seemingly endless crowds of faces from so many races that it seems the entire world has been forced between these grimy slums, there is a sense of a lot of people making something out of nothing. Through the city's two thousand Spiritist churches and legion Evangelical ones, the Paulistanos have shown that they will be nobody's underdog for ever. The power of the Catholic Church has waned, as the zero population growth shows. The monumental problems of the city are being tackled, often privately and by volunteers. Whether or not any solution can be found remains to be seen. It is hard to believe that such chaos can ever be accounted for, yet I find many enthusiastic people who are prepared to try. Perhaps my hotel maid sums up her city best when I ask her what São

Paulo means to her: she thinks hard and then shrugs, 'It's poverty . . . it's where I live.'

It is a relief to leave São Paulo behind me, although the train gives a last peep-show of the poverty as it dissects the endless suburbs and the lines of shanties. If the architects who built the city itself had shown half the imagination and powers of invention that the residents of the *favelas* have in the construction of their shacks, São Paulo would not be the grim nonentity it is. To escape from the anonymity street people write their names on walls, filling the city with graffiti.

When the first fields appear, latticed in morning glory, I relax. I am not doomed to stay on the outskirts of that drear place for ever. I become garrulous in my reprieve and get myself into a monarchy debate with two women near me. There is to be a national referendum on the monarchy. Other passengers join in and tell me they will all vote to bring back a king on the grounds that one corrupt leader is better than hundreds of them. In Bahia, they tell me, they want to elect an African king. 'What's your king like?' they ask me, as though he and I had just played marbles together.

My luggage consists of a map, a timetable, a hat, a small doctor's bag and an unnaturally heavy suitcase. My suitcase is filling up with trophies of wood and stone, and the timetable is increasingly more tyrannical the nearer it gets to the Mato Grosso do Sul. Trains there appear only twice a week, so most of the random stops I can allow myself have to be near the beginning. My inclination is to stop and wander all along the line, but I see reaching Bolivia as a challenge, so where the train rattles in and whistles out of unknown places, I hoard their names to add to the litany of stations I might visit one day: Jundiai, Louveira, Vinhedo, Valinhos, Santa Gertrudes, Batovi, Itirapina, Brotas, Dois Córregos. These are all battered signs and red-tiled station houses. A few are towns, but most are straggling villages of dusty streets lined with stray mangy dogs and old men, mango and lemon trees. Buzzing radios and flies throb out of them, as do the cries of children playing football on dried mud.

At each stop, someone gathers up their grimy plastic bags and their scattered chattels and climbs down. There are always more people on the station who catch the train. It seems to be a national pastime to stand and wave. Out of the banks of red-tasselled grass and the choking webs of morning glory, the signs of habitation often come unannounced. Passengers jolt in their sleep and then grab their possessions with a haste unwarranted by the lazy pace of the train. We jog along at a constantly interrupted twenty miles an hour. At level crossings, the train stops to let the road traffic by.

Beyond the sprawling factories of Jundiai, there are shock waves of high brick flues girdled by stacks of orange-red bricks. The earth itself is a startling tandoori red. Between neglected tracts of scrub and wild cane, the land is partitioned neatly into small vineyards.

At Campinas we make a five-minute stop. The platform is empty at one end and packed at the other, where more than fifty men, women and children laden with unwieldy bundles jostle to get on the train. What sounds like a fight turns out to be the labourers and the homeless making use of the two compartments on the end of some trains that are reserved for the very poor to travel free. 'They used to travel on the roof,' someone tells me. 'You'll see – they still do sometimes.' The two cars are packed with people sitting, standing and squatting in, on and under the seats. Through curiosity I nearly miss the train and have to jump back on to a free wagon where I am compressed against a nursing mother who tells me, 'The free travel is good, but you can't eat it.' Later she says, 'Yes, the medical care is all right . . . it's other things that are bad in Brazil.'

'Like?'

'Life. Life is hard and then you die . . . it's better not to think about it – just travel along.'

She turns her attention to her fretting baby. A little girl beckons to me. When I get to her, she whispers that she wants to know my name. Names are the most frequent questions, outstripping 'Do you like Brazil?' or whichever fraction of it I am standing on at the time. A name in a country with a population of 148 million people, of whom 25 million live in *favelas* and 12 million are abandoned children, is one of the few things everybody owns. I sense a genuine pleasure at the receipt of a name, my name, and an act of generosity in returning the favour – Rosa.

I'm on my way to Americana, caught by its name and hints of its history. The station itself gives no clues. Outside, waiting for a taxi in the sun, I am accosted by a floundering drunk demanding money for a train fare. His alternate threats and laments are so insistent that I dig into my purse and hand him a note. Far from appeasing him, this sends him into a frenzy and he starts shouting for hundreds of thousands of cruzeiros for his rail ticket home. With tens of thousands of cruzeiros to the pound, and inflation at 27 per cent per month, this is not an astronomical figure; but it is beyond either my budget or my inclination. A crowd gathers around us, appearing from nowhere. The general consensus of opinion is that I shouldn't have given him anything, that he's mad, 'a human leech'. The beggar takes the brunt of the abuse while I get lectured on not being a fool. Within seconds of being led away, he returns with renewed vigour.

I came to Americana to see a last stronghold of the Confederate Army. This is where they came to plant cotton and to die. There is an American cemetery beyond the town, where lie the descendants of those defeated families who freighted their pride and their possessions, medals and relics from the southern states of the USA to this southern state of Brazil.

Extricating myself with some further difficulty from the would-be traveller, I go in search of Judith Jones, born and bred in Americana of Confederate stock. Her garden is an oasis of orchids, her house a treasure trove of memorabilia. Later, I get my first baptism of dust on the way to the graveyard, bouncing along in a jeep over interminable red dirt tracks through fields of sugar cane. It is so far! The early funerals must have been like expeditions; I wonder who carried the coffins.

I slink back to the station disguised in a film of red dust. The beggar has given way to children selling chewing-gum and an old man with bleary cataracts measuring the inside of the building by pacing round it as obsessively as a mule on a treadmill. A russet goods train gurgles through, followed by the train to Bauru which limps in as scarred and bruised as the walking wounded, and then leaves at much the same pace.

This is the first chance I have had to spend more than a couple of hours on a Brazilian train. I am looking forward to the sheer distance to be covered and the chance to get to know the disparate strangers on the train with me as more than fleeting acquaintances. This opportunity is extended by a derailment at Cordeiropolis, less than an hour in. News of the derailment is greeted with resignation – it seems they happen all the time. All but the most ancient and most plastered of the passengers get out and stand around listening to the chorusing radios. It is oppressively hot; to move is to melt. The plastic seats give off a cocktail of smells ranging from sweat and rope to disinfectant. There are cholera warnings in every compartment.

By the time we eventually get moving, it is dusk; and then, within minutes, it is darkness, so the herds of hump-backed zebu cattle I'd heard about and the huge orange groves have been swallowed by the night. It is after ten when we finally get to Bauru.

This is a city that seems to be famous only for its fried egg sandwiches and a particularly itchy midge bite. As I wander through the city just before midnight with two former passengers in search of food, Bauru looks like a concrete *favela* drained of any colour or spontaneous form of life. We have been directed to a restaurant 'just round the corner' which turns out to be nearly an hour's walk away through miles of blue neon arcade. This is a boom town unashamedly modelled on American ways, achieving the shape without the essence. Even the hundreds of neon arches have a Disneyesque quality: uptown Bauru is there somewhere under the rainbow, but the depressive atmosphere is such that even the rainbow has got the blues.

My hotel is like a 1950s' plastic emporium. Instead of the room I expected I have a suite, which means that I get two rooms full of bulging plastic armchairs instead of one. The air-conditioning clatters out occasional puffs of tepid air which do next to nothing to lower the hothouse temperature of my near windowless rooms full of sweating plastic. It is hard to sleep, so I lie awake and try to work out why Bauru should make such a bad impression, seem so unfriendly and give such a sour taste. My dinner of pasta stewed in what I am sure must have been dirty dishwater and then mashed with boiled garlic cannot settle either. Most of our meal was untouched and then put out on the low restaurant wall on bits of paper for the homeless people to collect. 'So there are *gente do rúa* in Bauru?' The waiter was almost as unfriendly as the hotel receptionist, though, so I learned nothing more of Bauru and its ostentatious wealth and hidden poverty.

Later that morning, at the station, I discover that due to a series of derailments during the preceding weeks the passenger services to Campo Grande have been suspended indefinitely. Cross-examination of every railway employee I can find brings gory details of the nine accidents but no better news for the future. Bauru is less sinister by day, but it is no less depressing. I feel panic at the thought of being stuck here, of all places. I feel I want to cry. I dump my luggage and wander out into the pounding heat in search of a bar. After a large fried egg sandwich, I still feel that I want to cry. A burly barman tries to cheer me up. We talk; and he tells me that a month in Bauru is like a month in heaven; *and* there is a railway museum. Then he tells me what is coming to be the catchphrase of my journey: 'why go by train when there's a perfectly good bus?'

The railway museum is a little haven of loveliness separated from the rumbling traffic and the dreary prospect of the rest of the city by some token railings and a bed of miniature pink roses. It is closed, and while I wait for it to open I watch some half-naked men loading sacks on to a lorry in an open warehouse immediately across the road, and assess my situation.

I have been wanting to make this journey for so many years that I am resolved to make it now, no matter what. I know from my earlier meanderings in the Argentine and Brazil that the railways are fast falling into disrepair and lines are being closed down all the time. Having set out, though, I am determined to finish my chosen route, to which end I have enrolled my considerable stubbornness. My problem seems reassuringly small compared to those facing Aleixo Garcia in 1524 when he became the first European to traverse the Mato Grosso do Sul. I am conscious that the railway museum is adjacent to the railway station, from which a great deal of shouting and the occasional shunting of a goods train can be heard. There are goods trains to Campo Grande and goods trains to Corumbá . . .

I sift through the contents of the museum with a sense of relief; these objects of nostalgia are not to be my handful of dust. The curator assures me, as one railway enthusiast to another, that my journey shall go on. I leave behind me the bells and caps, levers, brakes and model trains to find Ovideo. Ovideo is an old railway worker to be found somewhere across the tracks and behind the workshops; Ovideo is the key to my journey, according to the curator. 'He's with his wife,' he says. Ovideo's wife turns out to be a 1904 steam engine which he once drove and now caresses. He moves slowly and carefully as though nursing a pain, but he smiles like a boy, despite his eighty-four years. He is travelling to Campo Grande on a freight train, escorting four carriages of antique rolling stock to be restored further along the line. Of course I can go with him, he says. 'We'll have a party, buy in some ice for the drinks and talk trains.' He is leaving in the evening, then stopping off at Araçatuba for a couple of days. By the time I leave Bauru it is with better memories, having spent a pleasant afternoon discussing life and the Western world with some of the railway workers from the sidings, sitting out in the heat consuming curling steak and egg rolls and iced drinks. Fried eggs, like freedom, are good for you.

After all my ungracious tourism, Bauru has come up trumps.

The potential disaster has become a boon. Ovideo and I are travelling in style in a train that looks like something straight out of the Wild West. He has worked on the railways since he was a boy, and he remembers the times when wild cats used to wait for the passengers at lonely stations and maul them to death. He remembers the steam trains from Campo Grande to Corumbá stopping in the swamp for stokers and passengers alike to get out and gather scrub to fuel the engine. He remembers the violence on the trains; the fights and the travelling bandits. His memories spill out while the train sways through the night. They are like the network of veins under his weathered parchment skin, feeding his frailty. He takes me from the dark wood-panelled sitting room with its blue glass and brass lights to a yellow striped verandah, where we sit until the plague of mosquitoes drives us back in.

'One of my friends was collecting tickets on this line . . . about forty years ago. There was a big man, a cowboy, with his hat and boots — big, though, bigger than me. My colleague asked him for his ticket. The man gave him a mean look, took out his knife, took out his ticket, stabbed it, and handed it like that at knife point. So my friend was very calm, he took out his gun, took the ticket off the knife, shot a hole in it and handed it back. Life was an adventure then.'

'And now?'

'Now it's a pleasure to remember.'

During the course of the evening Ovideo conjured up iced drinks and a bowl of apples, and a number of railwaymen who were also hitching a ride on the train would join us sheepishly for a few minutes and then slope off back down the long panelled corridor towards the other carriages and the engine. At around midnight we took our leave, I to my cabin and he to his. I shared mine with a host of mosquitoes.

We arrive at Araçatuba at four in the morning and clamber over the links of another freight train, hauling our luggage and the ice box towards a reception committee of three frantically yapping dogs. Somewhere near there is a frangipani tree which sustains me with its fragrance until a taxi arrives. I have two days to spend until Ovideo and I and the old train make our way to Campo Grande. Despite the music, bars and busy streets of Araçatuba, I decide to forgo any more urban experiences in favour of a rural ride.

Bob, an Anglo-Indian sometime painter who lives in a *favela* in Rio, and Ruço, his driver, who sports a blond ponytail and bare chest and drinks beer from breakfast to bedtime and whispers sweet nothings in every passing female's ear, have volunteered to accompany me to a sugar cane plantation. Having spent seven years growing sugar cane myself in the foothills of the Andes, I am intrigued to see how it is grown here. Sugar is big in Brazil; most of it is turned into alcohol and used as an alternative car fuel to petrol. This was good while oil prices were high, but is proving uneconomic in the slump.

The roads are the same red and the heat is smothering. Our first stop is at the sugar factory which stirs no nostalgia in me, bearing as much resemblance to the rustic factory I used to manage in Venezuela as a go-cart does to a jumbo jet, although doubtless the transition from grey cane juice to sugar crystals must intrinsically be the same. Although we have hardly finished eating an immense tropical breakfast (litres of orange juice and heaped bowls of sliced fruit eaten with a rubbery white cheese and all the delicacies of a Parisian patisserie), we are ushered into the factory canteen to do justice to a factory lunch. The menu of rice, manioc and *fejoada* (stewed beans), topped with a steak and a fried egg, is the same, dish for dish, as almost every other meal I have eaten so far in Brazil. Fortunately, I like all these stock national favourites, although I occasionally dispense with the egg. Ruço manages to stash away an industrial quantity of food while simultaneously chatting up the factory girls. After lunch, and a very long wait for the manager, we learn that this is not the cane cutting season in Araçatuba; but there is a field being cut for replanting 'just around the corner'.

An hour later, bone-shaken by Bob's ancient jeep and nearing dehydration, we crawl out from under the covering dust 'to see the cane'. To get here, we have driven through endless miles of sugar cane fields, each (even to my impartial eye) virtually identical to the next with their blocks of cane standing over nine feet (three metres) high and virtually turning the avenues between them into tunnels.

We stop by a team of ten workmen and their overseer. Watching these men and boys, swathed in protective rags, slashing their machete patterns into each individual cane, eschewing the leaves with their itchy hairs and saving only the best segments of the cane, all under a relentless sun, rigid with exhaustion and in constant fear of snakes and blade wounds, I see that the tyranny of the cane fields is international. Cutting cane must always be one of the worst jobs around. It is a job for migrant workers, of whom there are many, and desperadoes. The overseer provides over 30 gallons (150 litres) of water a day for the men to drink during their ten-hour shift, but they also bring their own. Our idle curiosity brings momentary respite to the field workers before they have to return to the dangerous drudgery of the cane, while we jolt back through the dust roads to the ostentatious wealth of the villas and the villettes of Araçatuba.

En route, we pause to replenish our supplies of water. Each town or village that I reach claims the highest temperature yet on my journey, always with a forecast for more roasting days to come further along the line. Out in the cane field, the overseer claimed proudly that the temperature was 112°F (44°C); Ruço said 107°F (42°C). All I know is that this is the hottest place I have ever been.

We stop in a village called Taveros that seems to consist almost entirely of bars. There is a small school building at one end of the village, some twenty straggling cottages and shacks strung together like beads on a chain by no fewer than five bars. Ruço is in his element. The beer begins to flow and the sleepy street shifts out of the dead hours of the afternoon and sends its emissaries to the corner bar at the small crossroads which could be interpreted as the heart of this small place. Dogs, children and drunks begin to converge. The gathering spills into the street, the street spills into outlying fields lined by giant acacia trees and burgundy-leaved mangos. Shouted above the smoochy rhythm of the radio, we are told, in the nicest possible way, to stay a while – there are drinks to be drunk and stories to be told; not much new happens in Taveros. We explain about the trains and the tracks and my railway journey. 'No problem,' comes a chorus round the bar. 'Taveros is a railway town too. The house with the well and the flowering trees is the old station house. You can see where the old line passed behind it – there, where the washing is.'

My interest in that particular ghost station proved to be ephemeral. Once my volunteer escort of giggling children pushed me through the wicket gate, all my attention went to the meticulously kept flower garden and the lady of the house, her almost cataleptic husband slumped in a chair, her severely crippled and flirtatious nephew and her momentarily absent daughters. She navigated me around her old station house and in and out of the affairs of her family. Her girls returned and stored their things away in the boxes under the beds of the one communal bedroom. After a couple of hours I wandered back to the bar, where a party atmosphere was getting going. The barman was playing a guitar, badly but with gusto. Someone was singing improvised rhyming couplets, and a couple of men were shuffle-dancing to the tune. As I left Iris and her family at the station house, I had given her the Brazilian equivalent of a twenty-pound note. She beamed and her black skin shone with pleasure. 'Thank you so much,' she said, kissing me again. 'You have given me money from your country. I shall treasure it and put it on my wall.' It took a while to explain to her that this 'foreign' note she had never seen was for her to spend after fifty years of never even setting eyes on anything more than a pittance.

When the time came to travel on to Campo Grande, Ovideo was waiting for me as planned by the beautiful Wild West train.

Then we travelled through hours and hours of cattle lands to this cowboy town that doesn't know if it's a Latin Dallas or an old-time Dodge City. It was built on its plateau this century to service a junction of the Trans-Brazil railway; to the north-west, the direction of my journey, lie the most extensive swamplands in the world, the Pantanal.

Campo Grande sells cowboy boots, whips and saddles, and everything that might be needed by a cattleman around his campfire. It is big and bustling and full of the sense of having only a little past but a big future. The two days I spend there are pleasant and friendly. In the evenings, the bars and restaurants are full of lively young couples and groups of big loud cowboys. There are signs everywhere advertising karaoke evenings. Here, as in São Paulo, there is a thriving Japanese community. It is in Campo Grande that I get my first opportunity to buy some presents for my children back in Italy – I hope they all like rawhide lassos.

When the twice-weekly passenger service leaves for Corumbá I am there in good time to board the train. The first break in my journey is at Miranda where I can spend three days before the next train takes me further on. Miranda is a lovely sleepy place nestling like a sloth in the swamplands. Waiting for some kind of transport to take me to my hotel, I learn more about it than I will ever have time to explore from the station-master's small, half-naked son. Inside the station, doves coo in the rafters and an ancient Tereno Indian sits as rigid as a sentinel outside the office. With his long white locks and pleated wrinkles he looks so wonderful I set up a photograph of him. This is not my natural forte and it takes me some time. Just when I feel it's right, he heaves himself to his feet. I ask him to stay a little longer, which he does only after everyone within a radius of a hundred yards has been called in to discuss this request. Eventually, grinning with a mouth empty of anything but two sabre teeth, he complies. Many hours later, when I double back to the station for something, I see that he is still sitting immobile by the office. He shows not a flicker of emotion, but asks in a thick Portuguese–Tereno mix, 'Can I go now?'

Through all the upheavals, scandals and loves of my life, there has always been a constant factor in my love of flowers; this has expanded to trees and birds and those places where they most naturally abound. The Pantanal swamp is larger than Britain, spreading across the Mato Grosso do Sul and the Bolivian and Paraguayan frontiers. It is famous for its stillness and beauty and is somewhere I have often dreamed of visiting. Miranda is surrounded by its flood plains. There are pools along the dusty streets matted with blue water hyacinths. At night I sit out under a palm thatch by the side of the road sipping water coconuts and listening to fishermen's tales superimposed on to anarchic choirs of tree frogs, cicadas and screeching night birds. By day I travel over bumpy dirt roads into the nature reserves.

One of the biggest and best organized of these is the Klabim estate, which has 65 square miles (17,000 hectares) full of birds and beasts. I get to ride for the first time in years to watch the Jabiru storks, which are the symbol of the Pantanal. These are the third largest flying birds in the world; their necks have orange and yellow pouches the size of shopping bags. The rarest of the birds I see are the hyacinth macaws, which are almost extinct but nest at Klabim's and fill the evening air with their graceful flight and flashes of brilliant blue and scarlet feathers. Large, ambling capybara graze in herds, each presided over by a dominant male the size of a sheep. By almost every stream there are cayman alligators which, I am told, are essential for the Pantanal. Without them, the piranha fish would devour every other water creature; only the caymans, or jacaré as they are called here, can prey on the vicious piranha. In the past the caymans were so intensively hunted for their valuable skins that they were in danger of extinction. Now they are protected by the Brazilian government and, rather than hunted, they are farmed.

I visited one such farm, run by a charming Lothario called, most appropriately, Angelo Delamore. He began his life in Bologna, dreamed of tropical hunting and wound up in Brazil where he used to shoot everything in sight on four legs. Then he saw the light and began to farm caymans. As he escorted me around his steaming pools of open-mouthed reptiles he assured me they were as meek as lambs – barring the occasional warning snap. However, as he showed me around the incubating sheds he told me several times that the same breed would instinctively bite anything that went near it. I survived both these tests and the impossible heat under the aluminium roof of the sheds, and then we sat out in a mere 107°F (42°C) under a mango tree and sifted through a box of sorry stuffed cayman heads, which seem to be all the rage in Asia as book ends and ornaments.

Apart from the lush vegetation, there has been little evidence of the rainy season which is still, officially, not over. On my second night in the Pantanal, returning via a circuitous route from the Klabim estate, I got caught in a thunderstorm. Within half an hour the road became impassable, and my driver dropped me at a fisherman's rest in what appeared to be the middle of nowhere. The rain beat down for so many hours that I eventually stayed there in a bare room designed for six fishermen. I slept surrounded by empty bunks and implacable mosquitoes, to rise at dawn beside a river cobwebbed by kingfishers. By 5 a.m., most of the fishermen had already gone.

No matter where I was landed in Brazil, everyone seemed overwhelmingly friendly. Apart from the cities of Bauru and São Paulo and the waste heap of Cubatão, there hasn't been a single place I would not gladly have been stranded in for anything up to a year. I feel at home here. More than anywhere I have been, I see that Brazil is a country where there are homes and homes; there may be a monopoly on wealth, but there is none on hospitality. And Miranda, with its vestiges of the Tereno Indian population, its three horse-drawn taxis, its high street with an air of having been interrupted in a siesta, its still heat, its exquisite grilled fish and its pots of guaraná powder (a local elixir) I shall always remember fondly.

The train from Miranda to Corumbá is in the usual battered state I have come to expect now. The turquoise plastic seats are redolent of the passing kingfishers. It is crowded and so hot that many of the passengers fall into catatonic sleeping positions within minutes of our departure. Gilmar Ruiz from the Brazilian Railways is escorting me to the frontier; he is a good travelling companion and a trove of railway information. He tells me that much of the rattling, rocking track I have covered in the earlier part of my journey was built that way by the British, who were paid by the mile of track they laid and so incorporated as many curves as possible. He points out the Salobra Bridge, finished in 1931. He even knows the singer-songwriter Paulo Simões and his song 'Trem do Pantanal', which he tells me has become the anthem of the Pantanal. At Salobra I was serenaded with this song and there was an attempt (quickly abandoned) to teach me it. Glossing over my musical deficiencies Paulo told me a story about having first travelled by train only when the bus he was in was stopped in the Pantanal and a corpse in a couple of sacks was manhandled into the aisle. He said the screaming, wailing and arguing over this corpse was such that it drove him to take the drastic step at 107°F (42°C) in the middle of no man's land. Gilmar is very matter of fact; he says buses have to accept corpses as part of their charter. Paulo describes his trauma at the uproar in the bus, the wailing and the smell, so vividly and at such length that he makes his conversion to trains sound truly epic. He took this same route I'm on, followed by the so-called Line of Death to Santa Cruz. I have the sweet tune of his song in my head as I too travel the last eleven-hour lap towards the Bolivian border also, 'Rumba Santa Cruz de la Sierra'.

Corumbá used to be a grand inland port, and its riverside architecture shows the fading remains of what might once have been foreign embassies. It has an elegance and a charm that somehow obscure much of what it has come to be today. Once renowned for its trade and its river traffic, it is now known for its drugs traffic and its unnatural abundance of pharmacies. The cocaine comes in from Bolivia, but much of it is cut in Corumbá. On the one hand there are fishermen casting their nets into the

Paraguay River, on the other there are ostentatious signs of wealth and the chic restaurants and boutiques that accompany them. Other shops are full of Pantanal souvenirs – stuffed piranha fish and feather necklaces and painted terracotta macaws. The streets are full of willing guides, many of whom seem more willing than they are experienced. Sitting out at night by the waterfront eating grilled dorado and toying with caipirinhas (the national drink of rum, limes and crushed ice) it is hard to assimilate the more sinister side of Corumbá. I finish off the evening with a stroll by the river. Somewhere above me some musicians are playing; it isn't the usual 'Let's jump up and dance' music – it has a more nostalgic feel to it, drifting over the water, merging into the calm of the night.

There is a long, dusty road between the frontier stations of Corumbá and Quijarro, its Bolivian equivalent. Somewhere in between there is an archway guarded by Bolivian frontier guards who look so young they are like children in uniform. The guards are jumpy and keep the immediate vicinity of the arch in perfect military order. On either side there are signs of squalor and people wheeling and dealing. Everyone eyes everyone else with suspicion on the bumpy taxi ride to Quijarro station, while the Indian families in the crumbling huts by the wayside look pointedly away under the meagre shade of their stunted papaya trees. After the wealth of Corumbá, the poverty of Quijarro is striking. Most of the passengers are carrying huge bundles wrapped in sacking or woven Indian cotton, trotting under their loads.

There is only one train today and the frontier formalities have allowed barely enough time to catch it. Minor miracles are taken for granted in the timetable, and distance is virtually ignored. There was a rail strike yesterday and there are fears of another. On the platform the train is already panting, and there is an air of panic. A doughy lady with waist-length plaits and swaddled in striped cotton is selling meat *empanadas* straight from a tin pan, but with the rush for the train and the heat her best customers seem to be flies. There are trolleys and carts selling the ubiquitous cinnamon-flavoured chewing gum, cigarettes and what look like devotional cigarette cards mixed in with a range of gaudy plastic miscellany.

My next stop is San José de Chiquitos, a Jesuit mission town founded by Father José de Arce in 1698 on the ruins of the original site of Santa Cruz. The roads that were once beaten by the Church militant and their indoctrinated Indian followers have closed over and there is now no proper road to San José. The Bolivian government took over the railroad on its completion in 1951, and it is along its narrow gauge that I shall go. I check the train twice and join the scrum. It is already overcrowded and waves of extra passengers are ramming themselves and their luggage into every available space. The carriages are dilapidated and beginning to rust. As I make my way past the jostle of vendors and passengers, I see that this is El Expresso del Oriente, the Orient Express – a train I have often fantasized about but never, somehow, in this guise.

Once on board, I find a place for my suitcase more easily than for myself. Up to a dozen people are clinging to the gaps between the carriages. I recognize several of them from Corumbá, including two middle-aged women who elbowed in front of me at the passport queue; they are laden with electric fans and other voluminous merchandise. The whistle blows, and people peel off from the doorways and windows like human scales; then the train chugs out into the Bolivian Pantanal. The soil, which has been anything from russet to porphyry all through Brazil, has changed suddenly to a dull brown, but the heat is no respecter of frontiers. Babies and toddlers shelter from it under the seats where mini-shanty towns are deftly constructed while most of the other travellers contrive to sleep.

A delightful lady in a blue overall and large white plastic earrings that rock with the train sweeps and mops at regular intervals, gathers all the Coca-Cola cans and Pacena beer cans into her dustpan and then deftly throws them out of the window. Through all the long hours of the trip she remains as cheerful and as immaculate as at the start, pulling cold drinks from her overall pockets and sluicing down the floors with a powerful disinfectant. The train, like the station, abounds with cholera warnings.

There are fewer flowers now in the dense greenery; patches of purple algodon still put in an appearance, and sometimes a clump of morning glory smothers its way over a bush, but mostly there are low green trees and solitary spiky palms. There seems to be no sign of habitation beyond the immediate vicinity of the tracks. Whatever homesteads there are huddle around the stations; everyone here waves at the train, and some of them seem to be wearing their Sunday best. Whenever the train stops for more than a few seconds, dozens of people jump off – only to jump on again as we jolt back into motion. Several times men have to chase after us and need to be assisted back on. Undaunted, they return to the trackside at the next halt.

In the distance, eerie rock formations loom into view and then are lost again. At Roboré the train is mobbed by infant vendors competing wildly to sell bags of shrivelled lemons. Oranges, orange juice, water and cardboard plates of cooked food are also on offer. After all the fish of the Pantanal it is a shock to return to what I had come to see as the stock Brazilian meal reappearing in Bolivia: rice, pasta, manioc, fried bananas, steak and beans topped with a tepid fried egg. There is no food on the train and it is to be a long journey, so I join the reaching hands and buy a plate of food which I then don't have the courage to eat. I also buy some oranges for later. The six-year-old orange vendor runs off with my ten Boliviano note, and then surprises me by reappearing in the train ten minutes later with nine Bolivianos in change.

There is an air of general excitement on board, bred by this sudden influx of food and drink following hours of inertia. News is exchanged noisily through the windows, vast quantities of water are consumed, and then we clang out of the station, rocking perilously, leaving a number of forlorn children still proffering their plates of food under congealing eggs.

Next come the dead hours, lulling the train into fitful sleep through the hottest part of the afternoon. Very occasionally, dwellers interrupt their siesta to make a few desultory, token waves from fading hammocks as we pass. Two little girls run up as the train pulls to a halt in what seems like the middle of nowhere, emerging from the swampy undergrowth with drooping ferns in their hands. They run alongside offering them for sale, and seem surprised when they get no response. Sometimes a snatch of transistor radio rises out of the undergrowth together with a thin trail of smoke. The sensual slur of Brazilian love songs and sambas has given way to the sharper beats of salsa.

The birds and the other wildlife must keep a calendar of their own: they seem to know which day the train comes through and keep a low profile in their otherwise unmolested swamp. After hours of looking out into the bush I only see two jabiru storks sitting in a tree, a lyre bird on a dying palm is preening its exquisite tail, and a number of hawks and vultures circle intermittently over the train as though waiting to see if any of the passengers will tire of clinging on to the hot railings and fall off.

My immediate neighbour, after treating me to several hours of suspicious stares, relaxes upon discovering that I speak Spanish and am not an American gringo. He comes from Santa Cruz and snores heavily in between drip-feeding me snippets of information about the wild cats and the Bolivian tiger. 'The tigers and the barbarians used to wait for the trains and attack the passengers . . . they were very exciting times,' he tells me wistfully. Apart from a silent battle with an Israeli tourist behind me for window space there is nothing of great excitement happening. The lady with the white earrings has passed again, leaving a wake of lavatory cleaner. Two men have an argument in the space between my carriage and the next, waking a baby and arousing the wrath of an otherwise mute woman. Then the dust settles in a gritty powder over everything, including my eyes and teeth. The sun begins to relent and the train slows down to approach San José de Chiquitos.

The station has a dreamy quality. The station-master's house spills into the booking hall and borders on to the platform. A trail of bars and shacks and an open-air restaurant sprawl down the platform and along the tracks in the other direction. A mutilated man in a wheelchair greets the train. He is an ex-railwayman who was crushed at his work. The station office is virtually empty, but the bars are full; this, I am assured, has nothing to do with the recent strike. Squat Indian women with long plaits and bundles on their backs pick their way through children playing and young girls stalking the bars.

I am staying on the main square of San José at a simple establishment, the Hotel Raquelita. My room is down a tiled alleyway and is almost as plain as a cell. But it is clean and more than adequate; and, best of all, it is mosquito-proof. This seems to be the only hotel and it is nearly full. The bathrooms are mostly communal, one for men and one for women, but I have been lucky and I have my own shower. When I turn on the water the light dims in my room. I discover later that the light dies in San José at night and the candle and matches by my bed which I first took for a charming touch are in fact a necessity.

Opposite the hotel stands the mission church and its compound, which look disproportionately big for the size of this sleepy town. It is built in stone, complete with campanile on its right and fortified gateway on its left, all linked by a high wall. Inside the church some hundred and fifty men, women and children are attending a weekday evening mass, all dressed up and with their black hair sleeked and wet. The responses, in Spanish, are said with real fervour. The scene presents a striking contrast to the lax or absent Catholicism of Brazil. The congregation stands between high pillars of tropical wood. There is scaffolding against the plastered walls and a purple-clad statue of Christ has a large cobweb on his crown.

Over dinner in a café inside someone's house – fried chicken and rice, followed by home-made ice cream with an undertow of rancid butter – I learn that a number of local people have been organized into a team of restorers and it is they who are preserving not only this but several other of the Jesuit missions.

Unlike the passengers on the train, the Chiquitanos are very friendly. By my first evening in Bolivia, I know that I want to stay longer.

My wish is all but granted next day: the rail services (scant as they are) have been disrupted by the strike and its aftermath and there is no train to Santa Cruz, nor will there be for some days. An afternoon spent carrying out an in-depth survey of the local brews and travelling possibilities provides a jigsaw of information. The new road to Santa Cruz is blocked by torrential rain. The old road takes anything from seventeen to twenty-seven hours through dangerous conditions, and everyone stares into their beer bottles at the mere mention of a lift. The station is open, but closed. Everyone has a different version of events, lengths of time, roads and tracks. At the point where dusk is all but falling and even the stray dogs have lost interest and dragged their scrawny carcasses away, and I am about to return to the old brick streets of San José, a freight train rattles into the station *en route* for Santa Cruz. So there were no trains at all – except for this. I am reminded of my farming days in the Andes, when my workmen, on being asked to do something, would say, 'I would do anything in the world for you – but not this.'

I am getting to be an old hand at riding on goods trains. This one is decked out like a hobo's boudoir with several sleeping mats, blankets and plastic bags of clothes. There are five railroad men in the cattle-truck carriage, all hugely amused by my wanting to share their discomfort. They have beer and little tins of condensed milk and some rather soft biscuits filled with a cloyingly sweet strawberry cream. Each time the train stops they wave a large, grubby, red handkerchief in the general direction of the driver; every time it starts again, we have a party.

Our meagre carriages hobble into Santa Cruz de la Sierra at eight o'clock in the morning. I am dropped at a siding. There seems to be a mistake somewhere, because the railway station looks like an international airport. This is the home town of Banzer, the ex-dictator of Bolivia whose name can be seen painted across every other house and tree; he curbed inflation and inflated Santa Cruz. The station is virtually empty – it has two trains a day – so its vaulted futuristic halls and its seemingly endless polished tracts of floors are peopled mostly by Mennonite farmers and their deathly pale wives, a handful of Quechua women and a troupe of cleaners who keep these floors immaculate and perilously shiny. The Mennonite sect is big in Bolivia. Founded in the seventeenth century in Switzerland, the Mennonites live by their religion in a time warp, growing fruit and vegetables for the cities of Bolivia. They speak only their own archaic Swiss dialect. They dress in the most curious old-fashioned garb – the men all wear blue dungarees and straw hats – they have huge families and they treat their women as a sub-human species. In the almost empty station hall at Santa Cruz, the Mennonite men with their unpleasantly suspicious stares add a sinister touch to the absurd dimensions of the station.

To arrive at Santa Cruz and think this station is a reflection of the city is to be over-optimistic; it is a reflection of the mushrooming and legally inexplicable wealth of this city, built neither on sand nor on rock but on the fine white powder of cocaine. The railway station is like a monument to that wealth; beyond it is a reminder of what Bolivia is like for the majority of Bolivians. Immediately outside the fenced and guarded station compound, a rutted dirt track full of deep puddles forms the main road into town. Cocaine is the country's biggest export, an estimated one in four working males works in the drug industry, there is a full-scale drugs war on, run by the US Drug Enforcement Agency (DEA) – so, understandably, drugs are not a subject that anyone wants to talk about. In fact, the only conversation I had in Santa Cruz about narcotics was when someone approached me wanting to know the exact size of my suitcase and where it would be leaving from!

Santa Cruz is a two-faced town. There is the almost grotesque wealth of the guarded villas, the hotels and the endless Toyota shops where stacks of Land Cruisers are for sale in a country that has hardly any roads. But then the Toyotas are not for travelling in – they are for cruising around Santa Cruz and showing off in, or maybe the rich buy them as garden ornaments. The other face is of a Spanish colonial city with its cathedral and its whitewashed arcades, its main square transited by every strand of the Indian races that go to make up Bolivia. In a flowering tree overhead, an unusually acrobatic sloth reaches for blossoms to the amusement of everyone in the square. Young women in elaborate make-up and costume jewellery drape over the benches chattering. They look at least twenty, but I am told they are about twelve. Santa Cruz, apparently, is famous for its precocious girls.

On the steps of the cathedral, a group of Positano Indians sit in their handwoven rags. They look extremely poor. The women and children beg; their language is their own, and all they have learnt in Santa Cruz is to stretch out their palms. They have been driven away from their tribal lands by drought. Now they have nothing; they are the poorest Indians there are. They huddle on the steps, chewing coca leaves. Their poverty and their chewing are a grim reminder that it was not the Bolivians who invented drug abuse: chewing coca has been a part of their very ancient civilization since it began. Is it Western sloth that is gutting Bolivia, I wonder? Meanwhile, the sloth in its tree is entertaining one and all.

Santa Cruz is the end of the line – there is no railway beyond it that connects in any way. So it is the end of my journey: a journey along a dying artery to the heart of South America. I knew when I set out that the artery was weak, but no matter how much blood is either starved or poisoned, the heart is strong.

HONG KONG TO MONGOLIA

Clive Anderson

Clive Anderson's journey from Hong Kong to Mongolia

Hong Kong and the Metropolitan Line

The first train ride on this great railway journey from Hong Kong to Ulaan Baatar was on the Metropolitan Line. Or rather it is on the Kowloon–Canton Railway, but the carriages on the KCR which runs from Hong Kong to the Chinese border are built by the British firm Metro-Cammell which also build the rolling stock for the London Underground. Its silver-grey carriages and automatic doors make the view over foreign fields forever Wembley Park. A prosaic beginning to an epic 2500-mile journey to Outer Mongolia.

Hong Kong itself does live up to its advance publicity. An oriental Manhattan, its skyscrapers from a distance have the same New York look of crystalline growth feeding on a culture of money. And the population of Hong Kong if anything outdoes that of New York for style and fashion. But why does it exist at all? Hong Kong as a bustling home to 6 million people is an accident – and an accident of history rather than geography. A twenty-first-century city built on an outpost of the British Empire. Too small to be given independence, too important to be given away, yet. Most of its land is held on a lease from the People's Republic of China which comes to an end in 1997, and the British government, having failed to bring it within the terms of the Leasehold Reform Act, have agreed to allow the Chinese government vacant possession after a hundred years of an economic miracle. Its prosperity is a triumph of English laissez-faire policy: letting Scotsmen run the place and getting the Cantonese to do the work.

Before boarding my train I tried to get the feel of the place. And it feels good. It feels prosperous and exciting. What it does not feel is panicky. The Communists are taking over in a few years' time but everybody seems to be expecting life to go on very much as before. Maybe all the panicky ones had gone already, but those I spoke to were anticipating business opportunities opening up for them and not fearing any clamp-down on their capitalist lifestyle. Maybe they have got to be optimistic. Hong Kong's wealth, once built on electronic goods and clothing, is now also based on finance. Making money out of money requires a special sort of faith. The Church of the Seventh Day Interest Rates. Confidence is required to keep you going. Like riding a unicycle, you have everything to fear in fear itself – that and falling flat on your face.

I went to the China Club to interview a number of the movers and shakers in the territory (the shakers and movers having gone to live in San Francisco or Canada long ago). The China Club is the brainchild of David Tang, a millionaire jet-setter who is on sufficiently good terms with the government of the People's Republic of China to have acquired the top few floors of the old Bank of China building, which they own, for his rich man's club. It has a balcony overlooking the New Bank of China building. This is an enormous construction whose threatening geometric shapes pointing directly at Government House presage bad tidings for the future of Sino-Hong Kongolese relations according to all experts in *feng shui*, the Chinese folklore of geomancy.

David Tang is not leaving Hong Kong. Or rather he is – he is on his way to New York the minute he has spoken to me, but he will be back next week. Hong Kong is his home. And his home from home is the China Club. It serves Chinese food in a Chinese dining room, but nevertheless has the flavour of a London gentlemen's club. What it does not have is the stuffy

heritage of the Hong Kong Club, the more established establishment for ex-pats, whose rules, I was informed, used to include
the listing 'No Dogs, No Chinese'. (Perhaps they did. I was told,
when I got there, that the same rules used to be posted in the
People's Park in Shanghai. Say what you like about the British
Empire, at least it was consistent.)

The Hon. Jimmy McGregor is a Scotsman also at home in
Hong Kong, though not usually in the China Club; he is only
there to meet me. Mr McGregor has a successful career in
banking and is active in the colony's scene. He is anxious to
secure the best for Hong Kong and its people, and one of the
few people I met on my trip with a good word to say about
Governor Chris Patten. Optimistic about the future, he points
out that capitalism is taking over in China before Communism
has a chance to take over Hong Kong. Chinese factories make
more or less everything that Hong Kong exports to the rest of
the world. Hong Kong companies are investing in the People's
Republic, buying it up before it can take them over to pull off a
capitalist reverse take-over.

China has acquiesced in Hong Kong's existence through all
the years of Cold Wars, Cultural Revolutions and Great Leaps
Forward. For decades it had supplied the territory with three-
quarters of its water and almost all of its food. So to destroy the
place, all the Chinese ever needed to do was to turn off the
water?

'No,' Mr McGregor corrected me. 'All they needed to do was
to say they were coming.'

Well, I had to be going. On my way I tried some investigative
reporting. The rich folks of Hong Kong employ Filipino maids
and children's nannies known as amahs. Sunday is their only day
off, and on Sunday mornings the amahs, who are Roman
Catholics, go to church. And in the afternoon they go nowhere
much, having nowhere much to go. They gather in a square in
the centre of town like a large flock of starlings, sitting, standing,
eating and gossiping. Some are young girls. Others are mothers
who have left their own families behind in the Philippines to

care for the children of their employers. They are paid, I had been told, reasonable if not generous wages. But are often treated rather unfeelingly: a tiny box room to sleep in, rare visits home, little leisure time and nothing to do when at leisure.

Emboldened by my camera crew, I arrived amongst them to ask about their working conditions. Scared by my camera crew, they declined to answer. Or when they did they had no complaints. They liked Hong Kong and had no problem being apart from their own children and were quite happy hanging about on Sunday afternoons. Laughing, smiling and chuckling, they utterly refused to reveal anything of the misery of their working conditions.

Anyway, to get to the station at Kowloon you have to leave Hong Kong Island. I crossed the harbour on the ferry, giving a last look at downtown Hong Kong. It is called on the map Victoria, though nobody while I was there ever called it that. The weather in March was misty – not cold exactly, but not tropical. Maybe the weather was responding to its history rather than its geography. It was more like Rothesay in September than Asia on the Tropic of Cancer. In Causeway Bay was the Royal Hong Kong Yacht Club and its marina, where yacht owners do what yacht owners like to do the world over: leave their yachts tied up and ignored for weeks on end.

From Kowloon I had to get a train to Lo Wu at the border with the People's Republic, and there seemed to be little chance of getting off to a false start as the destination of all the trains on the indicator board showed Lo Wu. The KCR was eighty years old a few years ago (I have the commemorative video to prove it) and, although it shows every sign of its British creators, unlike most lines in Britain it does run at a profit. The line was upgraded in the seventies and eighties. Originally a single track for steam trains to lumber their way through Hong Kong's empty New Territories to Canton, it is now a slick, overhead electric train service which carries commuters from the New Territories to the city centre, as well as providing a popular link with mainland China.

Once aboard and you travel the twenty-odd miles to the border you realize that Hong Kong is not just the famous central business area. Hong Kong is small and crowded, but not as crowded as all that. Apart from the sweaty inner city areas, there are also countryside, hills, seaside and little suburban towns. Last stop is Lo Wu, where you cross into China proper.

The People's Republic

Lo Wu on the Hong Kong side smells of pigs. Trainloads of live pigs are shipped into Hong Kong every day, their great railway journey being a one-way ticket to oblivion. The pig line runs alongside the human line, dominating the air. Incongruously, the maid in front of me as I queued to get out of the station was carrying a whole roast baby pig in a special carrier. Live pigs in, dead pigs out – it must mean something. Even more significant are the two pipes which also run alongside the tracks. One carries the fresh water into Hong Kong, the other takes her sewage back out again. This could be a metaphor for the way capitalism treats Communism, or the rich treat the poor. Or then again it could just be fair exchange: the sewage is used to fertilize the land.

Crossing the border is as problematic as crossing international borders the world over, but no more so. There are two forms to be filled in. Neither asks me if I am or have been a member of the Conservative Party. One does ask if I am suffering from any disease such as fainting or vomiting. It is somebody's job to print these forms; somebody else's to put them out on a desk; somebody else again's job to stamp them; and still somebody else after that's job to collect them in. It is nobody's job, as far as I can see, to actually read them. Nor does anybody check if they have been filled in accurately. Only a madman would reveal that he was suffering from a health problem if he wanted to get into the country. Perhaps that is what they are trying to do – keep out madmen.

Then there is the regular crossing-the-border form on which

you have to write down the number of your passport and where it was issued, the number of your visa and a selection of other bits of information about yourself. Some countries' Customs need to know where you are staying, others like to know what the object of your visit is. Most of them seem interested in what your job is. If you put 'smuggler', would anyone notice? It is my theory that there is an international cartel of paper manufacturers and printers which has all governments in its thrall and demands that every day millions of little bits of scrap paper are used to collect useless bits of information from travellers the world over.

In the queue to have my passport stamped by an official I bump into Jimmy Ng, a Chinese American who carries with him a photograph of himself standing with President Clinton. Damn. I have armed myself with photographs of my family in case I need to swap anecdotes with people I meet but I have accidentally forgotten to get my photograph taken with John Major (Prime Minister of the United Kingdom at the time of my journey).

Did I mention the smell? The actual border between Hong Kong and China is a little river – no, a creek – above which you walk on a bridge. A yellow line on the bridge marks the precise point at which sovereignty changes, and a stench of sewage wafts upwards to mark your rite of passage. It could be human sewage, it could be pig. Either way, let us face it, this is shit creek and I am up above it.

To be fair (and to reveal something of the intricacies of filming), the next day I had to go back to the border so that my walking into China could be captured on film by the camera crew positioned on a rooftop. Overnight there had been rain and the creek had been freshened up. Or maybe my nose had got accustomed to the pong. Whatever the reason, on that next day it did not seem so bad. This was just as well, because in order to film me crossing the bridge I had to go back to the very central point . . . to the yellow line in fact . . . and stand there at the smelliest point and wait patiently while the camera was readied. The officials of the People's Republic were extremely cooperative about taking me back through all the inspecting, stamping, guarding officials, but on no account was I allowed to cross the yellow line back into Hong Kong, or . . . well, perhaps I would need another visa, or maybe I would have to fill in another declaration about not vomiting . . . anyway, go to the yellow line and no further . . .

I knew nothing about China and I was hoping for it to be as different as possible from anything I had seen before. It is nice being somewhere like Hong Kong. The familiar, British things are in their own way exciting. A statue of Queen Victoria here, a Leyland bus there. The mundane things, the things in many ways you left home to get away from become interesting in a new context. But ultimately you want to get away from reminders of your homeland. Goodness only knows what Americans do to get away from it all. Every city on Earth now has its McDonald's, Marlboro cigarettes and Coca-Cola on the hoardings. No wonder they went to the Moon.

Well, I did find China very different, but not immediately. The border town is Shenzhen, which has been declared a special economic zone. Trade with the outside world is allowed, indeed encouraged. So when you leave the station, instead of walking into a brave new world of egalitarian conformity you find something which is to all intents and purposes a carbon copy of Hong Kong. There are large skyscrapers, industrial works, hotels and indeed Marlboro adverts. It has all been built in the last few years since the government in Beijing decided this was the way forward.

Just over the road from the station is the Shangri La Hotel. An impossibly grand island of luxury, it offers the sort of Western style virtually unaffordable in the West. In the vast marble entrance hall a woman toils all day mopping up any dribble or mark on the shining floor. Another man's job is permanently to wipe the smears from the plate glass window. Two uniformed doormen open the door as you approach it. At the lifts a man is employed to point to which of them has arrived to take you up.

On top of the hotel is a revolving restaurant from which we are able to film rotating views of the town, courtesy of the manager who, like most people doing well here, comes originally from Beijing. It is all very pleasant – but a revolving restaurant? If Chairman Mao were alive he would turn in his dining room.

In the evening I am to take the overnight train to Changsha, about 400 or 500 miles to the north. This train, like all Chinese trains, is extremely crowded and tickets are quite difficult to arrange, especially as I am travelling with a team of eight. Before getting on we had managed to book a compartment of four 'soft sleepers' and four 'hard sleepers'. We are not travelling light. The camera, the film stock and related bits of equipment occupy twenty or so heavy metal boxes which the camera assistant, Justin, and to a greater or lesser extent the rest of us have to lug on and off trains at every point. The equipment entirely fills our soft sleeper compartment, the door to which we can lock. And so it was our equipment which travelled soft sleeper, while we, the mere humans, travelled hard sleeper.

Hard sleepers are not that hard, but not that luxurious either. In hard sleepers the beds are not in compartments but arranged in bunks of three – upper, middle and lower – all opening directly on to the corridor of the train. Privacy is at a minimum. But the sheets and blankets are perfectly clean. Where standards of hygiene do fall down – though falling down is the last thing you would want to do – is in the lavatory. Public lavatories in China are of the hole-in-the-ground-and-squat style which is favoured in the East. On the train, the hole in the floor of the train allows ease of exit of all waste material directly on to the track. For some reason cleaning of these facilities is not regarded as a number one priority. Nor even a number two priority. Luckily my experience crossing the border has prepared me for the smell.

The restaurant car is a bit grubby as well, but, as I come to realize, the food produced on Chinese trains is of an incredibly high standard. Cooking is an art form in China. No intercity sizzlers here, nor sandwiches inspired by Sir Clement Freud, but a full five or six platefuls of carefully prepared hot food in interesting sauces, cooked in the cramped quarters of a train galley, to be shared in the Chinese way by the four people sitting at each table. Sitting alone is not allowed; the passengers sit in an orderly way or the waitresses go spare.

Capturing all this on film is not easy but the other diners are all happy to take part, and vastly amused that the waitresses change the tablecloths – for the very first time, the odd cynic claims, since he has been travelling on this line. As it happens, I am suffering the after-effects of a series of minor ailments – an eye infection, flu and an upset stomach from a rather dodgy Italian meal in a Hong Kong restaurant which together hampered the beginning of the trip – and I am not in the best frame of mind for tackling chicken's feet and sea slug with a side dish of tripe. But the camera is rolling, so I have to have a go.

But, as it also happens, the regular travellers on the train whom I joined at one of the tables are rather off their food as well, so instead we work our way through a bottle of Bai jiu, a popular white spirit drink. This is not particularly tasty at first, but, in the way of alcoholic drinks the world over, gets better the more you take. Just in case, I washed it down with a few beers. For some reason 'beer' is the only word in my limited Chinese vocabulary that the waitress understood. But that too is true the world over. Beer is one of the few words you can manage to learn in a foreign language and always bring to mind.

The spirit goes down and the spirits of my new-found companions go down with it. One in particular becomes more and more maudlin. Another passenger explains in passable English that he is hoping to study next year at UCLA in California. My companion moans that he cannot speak English. It is all because of the Cultural Revolution which robbed him of his chance to get a proper education. But for the Cultural Revolution he would not be a commercial traveller hacking up and down on this crowded train, but going abroad to America like that young chap there. I try to comfort him by pointing out that I cannot speak Chinese and I am, after all, in China. This does not cheer him up. But he wishes to toast Hong Kong. He has been there. What a wonderfully well-run place it is. And how well run Britain must be if that is how well Britain governs a distant colony. To stop myself getting maudlin I try another swig of White Spirit.

And so to bed. Claiming I am the worse for drink, the director insists on filming me getting into my top bunk. Despite my unfamiliarity with the arrangements, the movements of the train and my alleged over-indulgence, I manage the climb up the ladder expertly and without difficulty at my eighteenth attempt. If all this disturbed the Chinese passengers in the bunks underneath and beside me, they made no comment. Maybe all British travellers film each other eating, drinking and sleeping it off.

Early next morning I awake to a dawn chorus of the other passengers hawking and spitting. Spitting is a Chinese national pastime. Everybody, young and old, rich and poor, male and female seems to suffer from a chronic bronchial problem which gives rise to a perpetual need to clear the throat and spit on the ground in a way only seen in England on a Premier League football pitch.

Anyway, in the morning the corridor is alive with passengers coughing and wheezing their way along to use the washing facilities. The atmosphere is very relaxed and friendly. Each carriage has its attendant – a smartly dressed young woman who comes along regularly to top up vacuum flasks of hot water which are supplied to the passengers, each of whom brings a cup or jam jar with green tea leaves in order to maintain a constant supply of tea to drink. At a brief halt at a station I buy something which looks a bit like an uncooked roll of dough and which tastes, oddly enough, exactly like an uncooked roll of dough. The girl I had been sleeping above, if you see what I mean, offers me some sauce to cheer the roll up. This is a fiery chilli concoction which you might attempt with a late-night curry and six lagers but which seems a little strong for breakfast. The girl mimes the fact that the chilli will heat me up all the way through my digestive system. *Ha, ha, ha* . . . Is she being friendly or getting back at me because I kept her awake during the night?

Mao Now

Changsha is a bustling Chinese town where I made a slight diversion to visit Shaoshan, the birthplace of Chairman Mao. 'Bustling' is the minimum description of any of the places I visited in China. Crowded, teeming, pullulating . . . a whole thesaurus of there-are-lots-of-people-around words is needed to convey what a filled-up country it is. A quarter of the world's population live in China, and I think I bumped into most of them every day. I know that there are wide-open, mountainous regions in China where you probably would not see another human being for several seconds at a time. But everywhere I went was just teeming.

Even the countryside is crowded. Here in the south it is rice country. Little terraces of damp paddy fields, the water corralled into shape by elaborately maintained mud walls, are everywhere tended by patient peasant farm workers. There are no empty fields visited occasionally by one man and a tractor as you see in England. No prairies of wheat just quietly growing itself. No set aside. Everywhere there is something going on. A woman herding geese, a boy leading a pig, a man ploughing with an ox. People bending, people planting, people working in teams, people working on their own. People. The People's Republic of People.

There are more people in the towns – some busy, many more just hanging around like film extras waiting for something to do. Everywhere buildings are being put up as though they were rapidly rebuilding the place after a particularly destructive war. Instead of steel scaffolding poles, heavy-duty bamboo is used to hold the buildings up.

Mao Tse-tung (Mao Zedong as it is now spelt) was born in Shaoshan in 1893. His parents' house is now a museum to his memory. And to accommodate the pilgrims who used to visit this holy Communist shrine a magnificent station was built in the 1960s. On the way to Shaoshan I met Li Guoqing who at the time of the Cultural Revolution was a Red Guard. Now a fluent English speaker, he works in publishing. He had put his revolutionary fervour behind him and studied in Watford, England. He is on holiday for about a week from his work in Beijing. It is quite a trip for him to come to Mao Zedong's birthplace, which he is seeing for the first time. The Cultural Revolution was for him an odd time to look back on. Regrets? He has a few, but then again, he has to believe some good came of it all.

Shaoshan Station stands empty most of the day. Three million visitors a year used to throng through here. Now it is down to one train a day. As it approaches stirring music starts up, the staff make ready and we are welcomed to the station. It boasts (as I think the word is) a vast waiting room graced with large portraits of the Chairman and a forecourt which teems with life and minibuses for ten or twenty minutes after the arrival of the train, but after that stands rather forlorn. A holiday resort, after the holiday. Or maybe a party venue after the party is over.

A man cycles by with his son balanced on the crossbar. The little boy is dressed as a soldier, as popular an outfit for youngsters in today's China as little sailor suits were in Victorian England.

Actually the numbers of visitors are up again; but they are not Maoists now, they are tourists. The Mao residence is a substantial but simple country property. His father was a peasant who dealt in grain, made good, and doubled the size of his house by buying the adjoining property. A single storey of six or seven rather high-ceilinged rooms, it is simply furnished inside: a beaten earth or concreted floor, a four-poster bed here, some old kitchen equipment there, at the back an enclosure for the animals, in front a large pond. It is like visiting Burns's cottage in Ayrshire. An interesting insight into the life of a former time, but providing little clue as to why this particular home produced that particularly great man. I found a teacher taking around some schoolchildren. Enthusiastically she explained what a good boy and pupil Mao was, how such good behaviour leads to success.

'So,' I asked Li, 'is Mao still regarded as a great man in China?'

'Oh yes,' he assures me. 'But we recognize that he did make some mistakes.'

Amongst these mistakes could be ranked the Great Leap Forward, in which 35 million people died of famine, and the Cultural Revolution, which saw the persecution of all intellectuals and the destruction of as many manifestations of cultural life as the Red Guards could get their hands on. But the official line is that Mao was 70 per cent good and 30 per cent bad. For all I know, that is accurate. Now Stalin, what shall we say? Eighty per cent bad, 20 per cent good. And how would we mark Mrs Thatcher, Richard Nixon, Alec Douglas Home? I do not want to be controversial, but I dare say there is good and bad in everyone. Perhaps the trick is not to follow leaders when they are getting things that little bit wrong.

There are no *Thoughts of Chairman Mao* on sale at the row of souvenir stalls, but there are postcards of scenes of his life (posed later by actors) and a whole variety of cheap trinkets to commemorate your visit. Moneymakers in the temple to Communism. Mao's picture hangs from windscreens. This is not because lorry and taxi drivers hanker after the old days of the Cultural Revolution, but apparently there was once a road crash from which a van driver emerged unscathed while everyone else perished. His was the only vehicle to have had a picture of Mao hanging from the rear-view mirror. Hence, because of a Chinese urban myth, Mao Zedong lives on as St Christopher.

We stayed overnight in a Shaoshan boarding house. Dinner, served in a freezing cold dining room, is hot Szechuan food. Soup bubbled on a flame in the middle of the table as we picked our way through course after course of spicy food and discovered that the way to serve rice in restaurants in China is to deliver it in huge rectangular slabs to a side table. Breakfast is exactly the same, except that there is also some rice porridge served with sweetened milk. Rice porridge is as tasty as oatmeal porridge. I am sorry, but that is the best I can say for it.

Next stop is Shanghai.

Shanghai

I rather regret using up my thesaurus of there-are-a-lot-of-people words before getting to Shanghai. Shanghai is seriously busy. Coming from London, I am no country bumpkin myself. But in Shanghai every pavement bustles like Oxford Street in December. You turn a corner and it is Piccadilly on a Saturday night. You dodge down an alleyway and emerge into Wembley Way just after the Cup Final.

And what do all the people do in Shanghai? Well, most of them are currency dealers, or so it seems. The Shanghai greeting is 'Change your money?' Everywhere in the world with a dodgy currency whose dodginess is not reflected in the official exchange rate has an associated black market of unofficial money changers. But China has a special built-in extra opportunity for its spivs. They have two systems of money: Foreign Exchange Certificates (FEC), which are for the use of foreigners, and Renminbi (RMB), which are to be used by the Chinese. Both are denominated in Yuan. They are supposed to be of equal value, but in the way of these things FEC are in fact more valuable than RMB. If you spend FEC in the shops you are likely to get RMB in change. International hotels only accept FEC. To be honest, I did not take too much interest. If I wanted to be a currency dealer I could have got a job in the City of London. (Well, I might have been able to once.) But I dare say if you started with dollars you could get over the odds in FEC and then get over the odds in RMB, and the guys who approach tourists outside hotels make a good living out of such transactions. And why not? It keeps them off the street.

As was my duty as a tourist, I wandered down the Bund. This wide waterfront strand (officially called Zhongshan Dong Yilu) has a number of famous pre-war neoclassical buildings from

Shanghai's Western-controlled past. As a spectacle the buildings are a slight disappointment. The Western-ness of the architecture is no longer particularly remarkable in a homogenized world. The roadway itself is a busy thoroughfare with a wide pavement alongside the even wider reaches of the Huangpu River. I strolled along the promenade, my pale skin, camera, map and travel book being the only visible clues to the fact that I was not a local. I paused for a minute to take a look at the river and was immediately seized upon by Sam, a factory worker and part-time English-speaking guide.

You can meet Sam or his equivalent in every city in the world. He insisted that he could show me around. He pointed out interesting buildings, guided me to the pleasant Yuyuan Gardens where we took tea, told me where I should take photographs. Well, I did not really feel the need for a personal guide, and he even failed to be of real use when I prepared to photograph the guard outside the Town Hall. A quiet word from Sam would have warned me off. As it is, the guard hinted that it was not allowed by pointing his rifle at me. But in many ways it was good to be taken up by Sam. His expert English, he claimed, was learned entirely from the BBC World Service. How many millions are there who owe their education to broadcasts grudgingly paid for by the British Foreign Office? And what a fine education it is. Clearly what is required to improve British schools is to sack all the teachers and replace them with radio sets.

Sam works in an electronics factory and is not particularly happy in his work. He is entitled to practically no holidays, he cannot afford to marry or even to take out girls, who expect to be treated more generously than he can afford. He likes to come to the Bund to meet foreigners. He expects never to go to England or America. He just enjoys, he says, showing strangers around his city.

I knew there was a price to pay, literally, for this kindness, but when the price was demanded it was surprisingly small. He merely wishes to change 100 RMB into 100 FEC. One is worth a little less than £12, the other a little more. Unless I am missing something he cannot be making more than a couple of pounds on the deal. Can that be all he was after these last two or three hours? But it *is* what Sam was after, because immediately we have done the transaction he is off, having had enough English practice thank you very much.

There are beggars in China, but not the masses of cripples and sufferers you get in Africa or India. No more, in fact, than you see nowadays in London or New York. They can be quite persistent but, like all Chinese, they are very polite and not at all threatening. One boy struck it really lucky with me. I was being filmed as I emerged from the enormous new Shanghai Station, the camera getting shots of me from the rooftop of a multi-storey hotel. I walked along the concourse trying to soak up the local life. Country folk just arrived in the big city; taxi drivers offering their services, that kind of thing. The boy approached me, hand outstretched. I dug into my pocket and handed him some change and moved on.

But I had to go back and walk along the concourse again. The camera was not ready or something . . .

I repeat my walk. The boy catches me again, I dig deep in my pocket, this time handing over far too much, and on I go.

We have bad luck with this bit of film, and so I have to do it several more times. And each time the same boy approaches me, each time I have to reach nonchalantly into my pocket for him. Depending on what my hand happens to grab, the amount he gets varies from the equivalent of a skilled workman's weekly wage to a Texaco Star Token worth 1/1000th of a glass tumbler.

It is a lucky dip, but one in which he is always, to a greater or lesser extent, the winner. At no time does he show a flicker of surprise at meeting me so many times or question the wild variation in the size of my largesse. He continues to play the part of the beggar as though he knows he is on camera. He is a natural, a star. Do not, however, look out for him on the film. The point at which he stopped me, so it turned out, was not quite in shot. Later that day we visited the recently reopened stock exchange. In amongst the stockbrokers and Shanghaiway-men I am sure I saw the boy trading his new wealth.

Shanghai in the old days was known as the Paris of the East, Whore of China, Queen of the Orient. The City of Sobriquets is now home, depending on how you count them, to 6 million or 12 million people. Urban China has a positively Dickensian look to it – reckless expansion mixed with old-fashioned squalor. The engine of change is something that a Victorian industrialist or modern-day mandarin would label 'Progress'.

From another rooftop location at the junction of the Suzhou Creek and the Huangpu River in the centre of the city the view is not so much Dickensian as Turneresque. Barges chug up both branches of the waterway. Steam and smoke hang in the polluted air. Great factory chimneys and other modern edifices tower over backyard workshops. Somewhere in all this there must be opium dens and Sherlock Holmes.

More picturesque is the People's Park. This is a pleasant city park of trees, lawns and shrubbery, giving everyone a breath of comparatively fresh air in return for a modest admission price. In particular there is an area known as English Corner where people go to practise the English language. Elsewhere in the (crowded) park youngsters and oldsters exercise their bodies, stretching, and kicking in a variety of disciplines: karate, shintu and tai chi. I had a quick cup of tea (the ancient British art of Ty Phoo) and set off to show off my English. Seven-year-old boys, teenage girls and eighty-year-old men all want me for my vocabulary . . . '*Hello, where are you from? . . . What is the weather like in your country? . . . How are you? . . .*' the strange, bland liturgy of language students of all nations. An old man gets us all to sing 'Edelweiss' and 'Auld Lang Syne', breaching such peace as there is in the People's Park. And now something by the Sex Pistols? Perhaps not.

Someone with profound knowledge of Shanghai life is Tessa Johnson, a long-time resident of the city who works at the American Consulate. Originally from Virginia, she has a charm-ing penthouse flat in the old French concession district, built and administered by the French when Shanghai had been carved into areas by the various European powers. From her balcony she was able to point out the surviving blocks of colonial architecture now swamped by high-rise development. The Chinese, it seems, are not interested in the past, and certainly not that particular period of their past, but Miss Johnson has published books chronicling the extraordinary interiors and exteriors of buildings before they all disappear for ever.

The interior of her flat is a temple of chinoiserie, her identification with Chinese ways even going so far as to keep crickets as pets. (You carry them around in a little box and they chirrup to you.) But she also has a pet dachshund which she has called Lamb Chop – a dangerous name for it to have in a country where dogs are as likely to be regarded as a foodstuff as a friend.

That evening we went off to investigate the eating habits of the Chinese in an outdoor late-night food market. There is evidence of food as a passion in this country. Al fresco eating in the street is not limited to hamburgers and hot dogs (no offence, Lamb Chop) as it generally is in England: stall holders here produce an array of hot dumplings, noodles, soups and so on, plus a veritable menagerie of stir-fried bird life. I did my duty for the TV viewers and tucked into a whole quail, its head eyeing me as I ate it. Too late I noticed the sparrows I could have had to excite hostile letters of complaint from bird lovers the country over.

You cannot pretend that most Chinese dishes are particularly exotic any more, as Chinese food is already so popular all over Britain. But there is something exciting about eating on the floodlit street in Shanghai, in conditions of hygiene ungoverned by an EC directive. It is funny, though, how notions of hygiene vary. The street looked a bit grubby to our Western eyes, but when I shared a plate of dumplings with the film crew the fact that we all picked up a dumpling with our fingers, not using chopsticks, had all the Chinese on the street astonished, amused and, I think, revolted.

Shanghaied to Beijing

As befits a modern city, from Shanghai you can take a really modern train. Double-decker, clean carriages and bang on time it whisked us northwards as we sat in comfortable seats and watched the world go by. Even the passengers are superior: two beautiful sisters, a rich young Hong Kong business man travelling with his beautiful wife; a minister in the Malaysian government travelling with his beautiful daughter, a student at university in England. The people are beautiful, the train is beautiful – even, on this train, the loos are beautiful.

A few hours later we arrived at Nanjing and changed back on to the regular green trains – back to reality and on to Yanzhou. And from Yanzhou it is but a late-night bus ride to Qufu, the birthplace of Confucius. The bus ride is convincing evidence that it is better by rail.

Bicycles are very popular in China, but not bicycle lights. On the darkest of nights, on the busiest of roads, lights are seen as an optional extra. The bicycles are not seen at all. There is a fortune to be made by someone starting a joint-venture factory to make bicycle lights and batteries in China. All manufacturing would be done as a joint venture with the Chinese government, and in this case their involvement would be essential. Because once production was up and running a directive would have to be issued from the Ministry of Transport requiring all bicycles to have lights. There, a fortune for the taking. It is my idea, but I bet the Japanese do it first.

Invisible cyclists are just hundreds of the hazards to the motorist on the busy country roads. Trucks, handcarts, rickshaws and horse carts all compete for space. At first you cannot help being impressed by the way that, despite the highway anarchy, so many collisions are avoided. Then you cannot help noticing that so many collisions are not avoided. I think I came upon more accidents in three weeks in China than in thirty years in England. Some minor, some more serious. Either way they cause very little stir. A few vehicles ahead of us on a busy road a rickshaw driver was knocked down and apparently killed. Our driver hooted at the gathering crowd to get out of the way. On the night drive to Qufu there was a ghastly crash between a lorry and a cartload of donkeys. In the central reservation they were gathered, some dead, some injured, some just terrified.

Confucius was born in Qufu in 551 BC and he is still pretty big there today. Or rather he is big again. His descendants, the Kongs, had lived in splendid conditions in this town, rewarded, even unto the seventy-seventh generation, for the wisdom of his philosophical musings about morality, good government, respect for authority and reverence for the old. Confucianism itself was not respected by Communism and in 1949 Confucius's direct descendant decamped to Taiwan, breaking a two-thousand year tradition. In the Cultural Revolution historic artifacts and statues were torn down but, like Maoism, Confucianism is now back in favour – at any rate as a tourist attraction. Restored to much of their former glory are the Confucius Mansions, the Confucius Temple and the Confucius Forest, the ancient burial ground of the Kongs. I saw them all. I was even able to meet a seventy-seventh-generation descendant of Confucius, albeit one who traces his descent through a cadet line. As a tourist I was able to dress up in funny costumes to have my picture taken. What the wise old Confucius would have made of any of this is difficult to say, but I bought a book of his sayings and I have resolved to try to find out.

We rejoined the train at Jinan by making another perilous bus ride. My guidebook, the *Lonely Planet Guide to China*, is harsh in its assessment of Jinan: 'You'd be better off visiting the north pole in a snow storm.' I am not sure this is entirely fair. At any rate, it was not at all cold. I only really saw the railway station, so I am not in a position to challenge the assertion that there is not much to do in Jinan. The book claims that the German-built railway station is architecturally the most interesting place in the town, but the night I was there the station was being rebuilt and was hidden behind scaffolding. Business, though, was brisk.

What appeared to be the population of the entire region or a middling member state of the United Nations was at the station trying to get a ticket to ride. Outside, this took the form of a vast army of country folk sitting around with extensive luggage. Some were able to watch a large video set up to provide entertainment for the waiting crowds. Others were at a ticket office. At the head of a vast queue people were literally standing on each other's shoulders to try to get served. Inside, it took the form of more of the same. Everybody wants to get to the big city, but there just are not enough spaces on the trains to go round.

As a group, the film crew and myself provided excellent entertainment for the crowd. There are a number of physical features, quite commonly found in Westerners, which the Chinese find bizarre in the extreme, beards, large noses, large breasts, large bellies and blond hair being chief amongst them. It so happened that as a group we exhibited all of these phenomena. As a bonus we had our unfeasibly large amounts of camera equipment. So everywhere we went in China we attracted attention. A travelling freak show: lofty, beaky, beardie, busty, blondie, baldy and tubby and their tin boxes. Step right up. The Chinese way of showing interest is to come close and stare. There is no threat, no verbal communication, scarcely a titter. Just intent, if also rather blank, looks.

We had tickets booked on this train, and we provided our magnificent cabaret threading our way between the desperate and the bored would-be travellers to load our equipment on to it. Once the stuff was all loaded it was decided that I should be filmed making my way through the crowds. The train had the look of a train about to leave. At the door to each carriage, the smartly uniformed attendants were standing waiting for the signal to go. But according to the timetable there was another ten minutes, and so far the timetable had been utterly reliable.

And so I was filmed making my way through the huddled masses. Until suddenly a man in a uniform ordered us to stop filming. Now, uniforms in China are a very familiar sight.

Policemen and women, and soldiers of the People's Army, are everywhere. The many railway staff are also all in military-style outfits. And any number of other functionaries are kitted out in regulation clothing and badged with suitable marks of authority. Not that this is particularly oppressive. The uniforms are worn off duty as well as on. A soldier taking her two-year-old to the shop does not come across as all that threatening. And the uniforms have a slightly unreal quality to them. For a while I imagined it was something about the cut of the cloth that gave the uniform a slightly theatrical, even tawdry, air. But really it is the shoes. Everybody wears their own . . . So instead of soldiers and policemen in military boots they wander around in trainers and slip-ons or anything they happen to have. It looks more like the members of a chorus at a dress rehearsal waiting for the proper stage shoes to arrive.

Anyway, what with being used to uniforms, and not being frightened by them, and not being certain whether this was a railway official or the KGB, for whatever reason Mark, the director, and the cameraman, Keith, carried on filming, even though they had been told to stop. I carried on making my way through the crowds to the barrier until three things happened at once. The barrier was locked, the train departed and we were arrested. More precisely, Keith and Mark were bundled into a room and I was left to myself for a moment. Perhaps they thought I was not part of the conspiracy to film on railway premises without lawful excuse – the victim, maybe, of the excessive attentions of intrusive cameramen. Well, I thought, that would be quite a useful suggestion to make if the going got really rough. But for the moment I could not communicate anything because our Chinese speakers were both on the wrong side of the barrier. One had departed with all our luggage on the train, while the other was on the platform trying to get back through to help us.

For a short time it all got a little ugly. Great fun, you would imagine, for the crowds in the station to see this bunch of occidental weirdos taken down a peg or two. It cannot be every day a freak show is grabbed by the fuzz. The patient travellers continued to look on intently and impassively.

The camera and its film were saved from harm through being grabbed by our giant camera assistant, Justin; tempers cooled and eventually we were taken to an upstairs room. This was another enormous waiting room full of more crowds, and screened off it was a soft-class waiting area. The screens were the sort they use in hospitals to give a patient some privacy when he is about to die or have an enema. We were told to sit down while everything was sorted out. Were we under detention? Or were the uniformed men at the door just railway guards? We sat down while we hoped arrangements were being made by Jim, our English-speaking Chinese guide, who had rejoined us and then gone away with officials, to get us out of custody and on to another train – rail and bail, as it were.

Our equipment and luggage, meanwhile, were making their way to Beijing, again using our soft-class sleepers, with just Stephen, our other translator, and Tom Owen Edmunds, who was taking the photographs for this book. Our only comfort as we sat around in the early hours of the morning was to think that at least we would not have to unload it all at the end of this leg of the trip.

And so we sat, curious hard-class faces peering at us through the screens while we wondered what sort of journey we would eventually have. Our guards, railway or otherwise, fell asleep, Jim was away for hours negotiating our way forward, and, as it turned out, listening to dirty jokes. We finally got on a train at 2.30 in the morning. No hard feelings, Jinan, but it was good to get on board. Thumbing at random through the collection of Confucius's sayings when gabbling to the camera, I chanced upon this: 'The Master said, "I once spent a whole day without food and a whole night without sleep, in order to meditate. I found no advantage in it . . . it is better to learn."'

Quite.

Beijing

So, bleary-eyed, I arrived in Beijing. Or is it Peking? Such was my ignorance of matters Chinese before making this journey that I had no idea why Peking was nowadays often called Beijing. I assumed that it had some sort of political significance, like changing Rhodesia to Zimbabwe or Londonderry back to Derry. It is in fact rather less contentious than that. In 1958 a new system of writing Chinese words in roman characters was adopted. The Chinese capital emerged as Beijing. Under the previous system it had come out as Peking. Similarly Mao Tse-tung is now Mao Zedong. They were originally trying to encourage the use of roman letters in China, but progress seems to have been as slow as metrication in Britain and the idea petered out. But Beijing is clearly the name to use when you are actually there. (When in Roma, after all.) Peking Duck, though, sticks to its old name. I cannot say what Pekinese dogs like to be called in Beijing, as I did not see any.

Olympics 2000 were big when I was there. 'A New Open China Welcomes the Olympics', proclaim banners everywhere; propaganda for the locals and for the Olympic Committee, which recently visited. Everyone I spoke to was keen on Beijing winning the race for the Olympics, though one or two did point out that the untidy peasants who usually litter the station forecourt in their hundreds had been cleared away when the city was being inspected. All to no avail, of course. In the event, the compelling charms of Sydney, Australia, proved more competitive and, I suppose, more charming. And there is no reward for coming second. Beijing air, incidentally, is dusty and tiring (less so when the Olympic Committee was there, because everybody's fires were turned off).

I took a taxi from the railway station and my driver took me around Tiananmen Square, which is famous for being the largest city square in the world (as my driver pointed out) and for the crushed demonstration there in 1989 (as I pointed out). My driver is fairly relaxed about talking of such things but more concerned with the way the taxi trade is going. He is getting out of it and hopes to work for a large corporation as a chauffeur. The taxi trade has been rather undermined by cheaper minivan-taxis which are taking the cabbies' trade. (The minivan-taxis were something else that was introduced to help the Olympic bid.) But that is the important thing about foreign travel, to discover that taxi drivers have similar problems the world over.

Mao's portrait is hung over Tiananmen Gate at one end of the square. On one side of the square is his mausoleum. A queue which would gladden the heart of Madame Tussaud is waiting to view his dead body – in death, as in life, still pulling the crowds in Tiananmen Square. Everything is on this square – the Congress of People's Deputies and other state buildings. And just off it is a huge McDonald's. American hamburgers by Tiananmen Square symbolizes the new China. The official Chinese policy is to open up to the outside world, and opening up it is to big business and big money – but not to the big ideas the students were reaching towards in 1989. To allow in the McDonalds and Marlboros, but to suppress democracy, is, you might think, to take in the bath water but lock out the baby.

Of course, China before the Communist revolution was a highly ordered, centralized state. It was and is more of an empire than a single country. Its size and structure make it more like Europe might be if the Roman Empire had stayed in being and not fragmented into different states. The size of the organization to keep everything in being is extraordinary. Agriculture requires massive amounts of interlocking effort by millions of people. When the centre here cannot hold, millions starve. Perhaps it is natural in these circumstances for people to acquiesce in what the leaders decide and hope they get it right. Even learning to write in China predisposes the schoolchild towards obedience. There is not much room for learning by discovery, or pupil-led education, in the years at school it needs just to memorize the three or four thousand characters it takes to be considered literate.

I called in at a school, and in my role as expert speaker of English spoke English to a class full of teenagers learning the language with a view to a career in commerce. They were happy chattering about life in our respective countries, what young people do in their spare time and so on, but the moment the conversation strayed near to politics their ability to speak English suddenly evaporated. However, their teacher, Professor Yih, was arguably the most extraordinary man I met on the journey.

He had been part of the old guard involved in the founding of the new China. His duties had included reviewing the position of a writer condemned by Chairman Mao. Finding no fault, he had spoken his mind, stuck to his guns and sealed his fate. For twenty years he had been punished for this 'crime'. The first five were spent in a labour camp in the frozen north of China. He and his fellow prisoners were forced to work in the fields every day unless the temperature dropped to 38°C below freezing (− 36°F). For another fifteen years he had to live in the custody of peasants in the countryside. He emerged not a broken and bitter man, but a self-taught English-speaker and intellectual. Today his face sparkles with humour and interest and he is a lecturer at a variety of universities and institutes.

He had supported the students in Tiananmen Square, and had been there to speak to them during their protests. He imagines the authorities would not choose to punish him further for this exercise of free speech. He had in fact eventually advised the students to give up their protest before what he saw as the inevitable crackdown occurred. But even this determinedly honourable man was not burning to see democracy established in China. Indeed, his greatest fear for his country was that Deng Xiaoping might die too soon. A holder now of no official office, Deng is credited with bringing forward the economic reforms.

In the company of Professor Yih I wandered around the dusty squares of central Beijing. It was early spring, and the weather was warm enough for the old men to gather in the squares and parks on Sunday. They seemed not to have any old women with them, but many had brought their pet birds, in their cages, for a breath of fresh air. The men sang snatches of wailing Beijing opera and played old tunes on ancient stringed instruments.

These old men all took the party line on such matters as Chris Patten and Hong Kong. Only one, who had been there, praised Hong Kong and suggested it was right that what was good about it should be preserved. They were certain that Chinese people did not like living apart from the main body of China. This is politically correct in Beijing, but ignores the fact that the population in Taiwan and Hong Kong is largely made up of Chinamen voting with their feet to get there. But, retired working men themselves, they were more interested in discovering what proportion of a British worker's wages would be spent on food, housing and clothing. I had no idea – I have never been good with my own finances, let alone everyone else's. My answer that it depended on how much the worker earned just puzzled them. Does not everyone get the same? So I tried a light-hearted comment that people the world over tended to spend whatever money they had. Oh no, not in China, they assured me. Chinese people save their money.

Even further off the beaten track, I went for a bicycle ride around the back streets of Beijing with Li, the ex-Red Guard I had met at Mao's birthplace. He took me to the house, a tiny couple of rooms off a back courtyard, where he started his married life, and where his brother and his wife now live. The rent is low but the conditions are rudimentary. A tap in the courtyard is where several families do their washing. The public lavatories a couple of courtyards away on the street are for more fundamental ablutions.

On our ride round we come across row after row of little shops, stalls and businesses which look as though they have been going for years, unaffected perhaps by political events. In fact, Li tells me, they are all new, having grown up only since controls on private enterprise have been relaxed. Filming in the streets is fun. Small children come to mug at the camera, but we are interrupted by a local Dogberry whose permission to film had not been sought. He is even dubious about Li allowing the cameras into his own brother's house. He would have given permission had he been given proper notice. Come the counter-revolution he will be working as a car park attendant.

Great Wall, Shame About the Crowds

The train north from Beijing takes you to the Great Wall. It is often asserted, rather implausibly, that the Great Wall of China is the only man-made object visible from outer space. Whatever the truth of that, it is certainly something you have to see if you are in China on your way to Outer Mongolia.

The Wall was originally built to keep the barbarians out, but now pulls the punters in. At Badaling it is at its most touristy with cable cars, souvenir stalls, coach parks, restaurants – the lot. The large, functional restaurant served, as usual in China, an excellent lunch. At the most upmarket souvenir shop there West met East. A blue-rinse lady American was explaining patiently to her Chinese tour guide why she was buying a model elephant. It is the symbol of a political party, you see, the Republicans. As opposed to the Democrats, who have a donkey . . . Whether the guide saw or not, she was prepared to help make the purchase. American democracy is incomprehensible. American dollars make sense.

The Wall itself is impressive in scale, snaking to the horizon over roller-coaster hills. And up and down you can now march, and buy a certificate to prove you have been there. It was first erected about two thousand years ago, then rebuilt during the Ming Dynasty which ended in 1644. But this section was restored in the 1950s, so it has a rather inauthentic look – rather like the Tower of London, which, because it is so well maintained, does not look like a real ancient ruin.

The regulations for paying to go on to the Wall are interesting to anyone fascinated by the self-deception of the Chinese state. Taiwanese and people from Hong Kong (who both visit the Wall in great numbers) are officially regarded as being just as Chinese as any citizen of the People's Republic. But citizens of the People's Republic pay in RMB. Foreigners and 'compatriots from Hong Kong and Taiwan' are required to pay in FEC.

At the tiny Qinglogqiao Station, where the train has to reverse in and out to get up the mountainside, the Wall is gazed upon by the statue of Chian Tianyu. Dressed in a frock-coat he looks exactly what he was, a Chinese Isambard Kingdom Brunel who had brought the railways to this part of the country, the first Chinaman to emulate the European railway constructors. His station is a strange place. (Even stranger is that there is another station nearby with the same name.) No made-up road leads there. The easiest way to get to it on foot involves walking along the railway track, even following it through a tunnel. This we had to do for the purposes of filming. It is a somewhat unsavoury business. The trains, quite apart from the waste products that drip from their lavatories, leave a trail of other litter in their wake. Meals on trains used to be consumed in carriages from metal dishes which were returned to be washed. Now they come in polystyrene containers like fast food does in all parts of the world. And as in all parts of the world the containers are thrown away. In this case, out of the train windows. Thus all the way along all stretches of the Chinese railway system are piles of rubbish. Even Chian Tianyu's station is knee deep in it.

Chian pointed our way to Datong, the last town we were to visit in China. A coal and railway town, Datong is where they build much of China's rolling stock – so it was obviously a place to visit in the course of our railway journey. (Actually most of the engines pulling the trains were built in Romania, but it did not seem worth going there as well.) It is a famously coal-dust-polluted city, but in the perverse way of the weather on this trip it was bright and sunny while I was there and there was scarcely any sulphurous coal smoke in the air. Datong lies in an area of the country which seemed, as we passed through it on the train at the end of March, to be entirely constructed of mud. Muddy fields, mud walls, mud houses. One good downpour and you feel the whole place would wash away.

Datong's railway factory cheerfully accepts visitors to see carriages being made in stages from molten metal to complete units, unhampered by some of the more intrusive safety regulations which are such a check on productivity in England. The factory has an outdoor museum featuring a number of locomotive units of historic interest now rusting away. The engine of the Emperor's train has coupling at the front only – because no one, not even an engine driver, could precede him; so the Emperor's carriage always had to be pushed from behind. The factory apparently sells marvellous metal scale models of its trains, but on the day we visited it the man with the key to the model shop was not there.

Datong had its glory days at the time of the Northern Wei Dynasty in the fifth century, and dating from that time are the magnificent Yungang Buddhist caves. These feature statues and carvings of Buddha cut into the caves at the foot of Wuzhoushan mountain, which now sit overlooking an industrial wasteland. Actually on the day I was there it was glorious. The sun was shining, the air fresh and the terraces leading to the caves were enjoyed by the few Chinese tourists who were having a look around. On the way back to the station the men were playing pool at tables set out in the sunshine and pigs rootled around in rubbish at the corner of a car park. It all seemed strangely relaxed.

Back on the train for the final stretch to the Mongolian border, I tried to sort out my reactions to China. It is difficult to know what to make of it. Coming across peasants ploughing fields with oxen, it is tempting to think of it as a third world country. And yet it has an ancient civilization and literate people, and shows every sign of an expanding economy. But as soon as you start thinking of it as a first world country you bump into something which reminds you that it remains governed by a second world Communist dictatorship. Perhaps it is not first, second or third world, but a world apart. I wanted to find something different, and different it certainly is.

The people were very friendly and even officials, whom the

guidebooks warned can be very uncooperative, seemed, with very few exceptions, eager to please. I never felt there was a chance of anything getting stolen, but I could not say if that was down to my naivety, their honesty or the rumoured existence of a death penalty for stealing from foreigners.

Mongolia

If I knew little about China, Mongolia was a trip into the complete unknown. Outer Mongolia is one of the classically remote places in popular British imagination, up there with Timbuktu and the back of beyond. Part of the problem is being called *Outer* Mongolia. Sensibly, the Mongolian People's Republic does not use 'Outer' any more, though there is still an Inner Mongolia, which is a semi-autonomous region of China. In fact, more ethnic Mongolians live in China than in Mongolia.

The train to Ulaan Baatar, the capital of Mongolia, goes straight on to Moscow. It has the same green Romanian-built Chinese compartments we had got used to on the journey through China. Datong to UB (as we old Mongolia hands call it) is scheduled to take about twenty-four hours, and luckily we had booked a soft sleeper for the long trek. Mind you, on the train are some intrepid travellers making the journey all the way to Moscow. A middle-aged couple from England who had taken a year out to travel round the world (starting with a walk from John O'Groats to Land's End) are on their way back from Australia. A Chinese businessman is on his way to set up an office in Russia, taking with him his new trilingual secretary in her first job after university. And there is a fantastic collection of backpackers, commercial travellers and, so it is said, any number of illicit traders smuggling silk and other goods to the crumbling Russian economy.

Also on the train are John and Maurice, Queen's Messengers. The Queen's Messenger's job is to travel the world carrying diplomatic baggage to our embassies. Most places they fly. In fact everywhere they fly except to Ulaan Baatar. This is the last journey Her Majesty's messengers travel by train, with their mysterious bulky white canvas bags which are never let out of their sight. Queen's Messengers do not trust the food in the restaurant car and invite us to a slap-up picnic in their first-class (which means even softer than soft) compartment. They supply Naafi corned beef from Hong Kong, John's wife's gingerbread, and cans of British beer.

But all in all this is the most exciting part of the whole journey as the train rumbles on towards night and the Mongolian border. The countryside has been mountainous, and is steadily getting ready to be the Gobi Desert.

We get to the border at about nine o'clock in the evening and finally get clear of it at about 2.30 in the morning. First the Chinese Customs officers come on the train in great numbers and take away everybody's passport to be inspected, and perhaps photocopied. (The Queen's Messengers had many a tale to tell of border-crossing difficulties in the past.) A few vital facts have to be inserted on an exit document (this is where we came in). There is no particular difficulty except for a couple of Chinese travellers whose suspiciously large amounts of luggage mark them out as possible smugglers. They and their bundles are bundled from the train. Later, though, they are allowed back on board.

The next stage is to change the bogies. Mongolian Railways have a different gauge from Chinese, so the train has to be divided up and carriage by carriage hoisted into the air while the wheel units are lifted out and replaced. This is all done in a freezing cold shed by impressively substantial equipment and a hard-working staff of young women.

Mongolian Customs then have to be negotiated. This involves rather fewer officers than on the Chinese side, but about the same amount of time. But eventually, five hours after we arrived at the border, the train sets off and we are able to climb into our bunks.

The next morning the train was passing through the noble landscape of the Gobi Desert. It was the beginning of April.

There were still patches of snow here and there and the spring vegetation was not quite ready to green the grey-brown landscape. Taking off from the fence posts alongside the railway line were steppe eagles flying in search of marmots – giant, furry, guinea-pig-style animals which were to be seen here and there scampering over the sandy ground. Occasionally in the distance I caught sight of gazelles. More frequently there were herds of sheep and cattle tended by mounted herdsmen, riding standing upright in the stirrups, which is the Mongol way. Here and there were collections of Mongolian yurts or gers, their traditional circular, tent-like homes. Occasionally the train passed more permanent settlements, and ugly military structures put up by the Russians.

But mostly there is just space – empty country which comes as some relief after the claustrophobic crowds of China. Scarcely more than 2 million people live in Mongolia's 604,000 square miles; 6 million people live in Hong Kong's 416 square miles.

At the border the Chinese restaurant car had been replaced by a Mongolian restaurant car. The Chinese are famous for their food. The Mongolians are infamous for theirs. Certainly the Chinese train attendants react to the change in catering arrangements much as French conductors would on being forced to sample British fare at its worst. They decline to visit the buffet and start cooking their own food – dumplings – on the heating stoves in their compartments. So I found the Mongolian buffet empty except for a mixed foursome of Americans and Englishmen, and a peeved group of Russians. All of us raised in the Anglo-Saxon tradition of culinary triumphs tucked into some 'Borscht' (Scotch broth with stringy meat) and Beef Stroganoff (stringy meat with rice). The peeved Russians had not been served by the time we left. The Mongolians are not well disposed towards the Russians.

Several hours late the train made its way into Ulaan Baatar from the high ground which surrounds it. Hold-ups at the border always delay this train, apparently, but we had had a further wait at Chory, a small town about 100 miles from the capital, where a new engine had to be hitched on as ours had run out of fuel.

Ulaan Baatar is the far end of my journey, but in many ways it feels like coming home. By way of welcome, boys on the platform are trying to get our luggage. They are not just staring like they had done in China, they are looking for something to steal. Hey, this could be London. In fact I took an immediate liking to Mongolia and the Mongolians. A proud people, they remember their past glories as a great empire when they ruled half the world. They live in a cold northerly country with a crumbling economy, bad food and an uncertain future. Hey, this could be Britain.

We missed the worst of the snow but it was still some way below freezing, which is just as well since I had brought special cold-weather clothing all the way from Hong Kong and I would have been disappointed not to have used it. To keep warm the Mongolians keep their heads covered – with fur hats or, in town, trilbies which, together with overcoats, give the men a rather 1940s' gangster look. Both men and women often wear knee-length leather boots. Though intended as practical wear, they look very sexy on the women and lend a certain swagger to the men.

The one international hotel is a large Soviet-style creation with high ceilings and unreliable heating. Up and down its central staircase wafts the smell of cooking meat. But then everything and everybody in Mongolia smells of meat: fried mutton with just a hint of beef. A nomadic people, traditionally they followed their cattle. Food was always meat in winter, dairy produce in summer. Vegetable cultivation was for wimps.

At one end of town a power station belches out black smoke as it attempts to provide enough power to keep everything going. It is a piece of old Russian technology, but now the old Russians have left and it is always touch and go whether the plant can make it through another winter. The Russians withdrew about three years ago and although that means the man who knows how to run the power station has gone – together, apparently, with the man who knows how to fix broken windows, and the man who mends the streets – they are glad to see the back of them. Mongolia had been Communist for about as long as anywhere in the world. The revolution had been welcomed as a means of throwing off Chinese domination, but collectivization and destruction of its Buddhist monasteries wrought the usual havoc in the structure of Mongolian society.

High on a hill is a massive memorial to great Soviet achievements. Protected by a round-the-clock guard while the Russians were still in charge, it now stands slowly falling to bits, unloved and untended. *Look on my works, ye Mighty, and despair!*

So now capitalism is going to save the country. On the vast Sukhbaatar Square there is a stock exchange established by an energetic young man called Naidansurengiin Zolzhargal. The exchange is in a former children's cinema and is heated and fitted out as though it was in hailing distance of Madison Avenue. Everybody in the country has been allocated vouchers to buy shares and trading has commenced, the computers coping not so much with heavy trade as with the vagaries of the electricity supply. Not that Mr Zolzhargal was going to be condescended to by me. A hint of doubt about the possibilities of success, and he gleefully reminded me of the London Stock Exchange's recent difficulties with its Taurus computerization.

Money, though, in Mongolia remains a problem. China has two types of money, FEC and RMB, but Mongolia has only one: the US dollar. Well, there is the Mongolian tughrig, but it is sadly not worth the paper it is printed on. Shopping customs are relaxed. While I was trying on a hat in the city's department store a fellow shopper offered me a better one at a quarter of the price and sold it to me in front of an unconcerned shop assistant. Try that in Harrods.

Late night our hotel bar is like a Wild West saloon, filled by middle-aged foreign business men out for a good time, and Mongolian girls out to provide it. A party of Frenchmen have been in Ulaan Baatar for months. They are familiar with the local customs, the local vodka (*archi*) and the local girls. This is a chance I cannot miss and I stay up late, practising my French.

Mongolia apparently has oil and minerals, and once they work out a way of getting the stuff out of the ground and delivered to somebody with a hard currency they will be rich. Meanwhile they trade in furs and agricultural produce and are utterly charming. Mr Nambaryn Enkybayar, the Minister of Culture, was especially so. When I interviewed him his description of the inside of a ger made us determined to film one. We were leaving the next day, but on the outskirts of Ulaan Baatar are a number of gers each inside its wooden stockade. At the first one we called at, completely unannounced and unarranged, we were immediately invited in, cameras and all.

A young married couple and their children had all been sitting around in their underwear, but happily got dressed and allowed us to film. Inside the ger, a fire in the middle of the single circular room keeps the place warm. Smoke escapes through a hole in the roof. It is very snug; the wooden frame supports a felt outer covering. It is a cross between a tent, a gypsy caravan, a mobile home and a house. As they are in town they have electricity, lighting and a TV to go with it, and comfortable chairs and that neat look of the inside of a small ship's cabin. But what they have is not so important as the fact that they welcomed us in at all. A Mongolian film crew would have to be lucky to be treated so well in Britain.

As it was, I had travelled 2500 miles by rail to visit perfect strangers in their own home. I do not know what they thought of us, but for me, it made the whole trip worthwhile.

ST PETERSBURG TO TASHKENT

Natalia Makarova

AT HOME

And that happy phrase – at home
Is known to no one now,
Everyone gazes from some foreign window,
Some from New York, some from Tashkent,
And bitter is the air of banishment
Like poisoned wine.

Anna Akhmatova

Natalia Makarova's journey from St Petersburg to Tashkent

It is given to few to alter the circumstances of their lives as fundamentally as I have done. Since my birth in Tchaikovsky Street in Leningrad I have known the war, the blockade and Stalin; I have known poverty and starvation, and spent tedious hours in endless queues; and I have known fame and the adulation of crowds, marriage, motherhood and material well-being in the West. The contrasts still subdue me and render me thoughtful.

As a young ballerina in the Kirov company, I defected while on a tour to London in 1970. I have told elsewhere the compelling artistic considerations which drove me to take this drastic step, to break with my family, my country, my past, everything that was familiar and secure, to plunge into an uncertain future. Suffice it to say here that I knew the decision to be final. It was inconceivable that I should ever see Russia or my mother again.

After nearly twenty years, with the advent of perestroika and the opening of windows upon a stultifying society, the impossible occurred. I was the first artistic exile to be allowed to return and even to perform in my native land again. That event, in 1989, was the most dramatic and emotional of my life, a tearful reunion with my family and friends on the very steps of the aircraft, grateful recognition from strangers, and a performance on my beloved Kirov stage which affected me as deeply as any that I have given. Since then I have been back more than once, and have begun to accept the normality of travel.

This trip, however, is different, for two distinct reasons. I am to undertake a journey for a BBC film which will take me to parts of Central Asia that I have never seen, to start from the city of my birth and venture outward and beyond, observing my own country through the windows of a train, discovering it anew. Secondly, I am accompanied by my husband Edward and my fifteen-year-old son Andrusha, for whom I must be guide and prism, sharing their experience yet interpreting it in the light of my own understanding of what they see.

There is a perfect balance between Andrusha and myself. He is an all-American boy and therefore remorselessly materialistic. I was brought up very differently, and taught never to attach too much importance to material things – that, indeed, is how I was able to survive. In Russia now people are struggling to adapt to foreign concepts of capitalism, materialism and democracy – the very freedoms that Andrusha has grown up with and naturally takes for granted. It will be an education for him to see for himself how a people thirsty for freedom cope with disappointment and frustration as they discover the nature and demands of these new values. Together we shall feel and experience my native land – my poor, beautiful, wounded and wonderful native land.

St Petersburg

I cannot get used to this name – probably because I spent the first twenty-eight years of my life here, when it was called Leningrad. In my memory it still is Leningrad, a city of eternally clouded skies and magnificent white nights. So far it has not yet regained the splendour of an imperial capital – it has not yet become St Petersburg, the ghost-city, 'the most deliberate city on earth', as Fyodor Dostoyevsky called it. It has become stuck halfway between two ages and two names, neither of which is appropriate today. I am at a loss. I don't understand my city, I don't know what to call it, this city of fogs and rains which fall all year round, in June as well as December.

It is a city of canals and rivers, small and large bridges with gilt lions holding gilt chains, a city of wide prospects straight as arrows and spacious squares aptly called 'fields'. I love it. I love its granite, its pale yellow-and-white façades that melt into winter frosts and June twilight, its famous palaces, and even the sombre light of back yards and back stairs that smell of poverty and cats. After all these years it has never eased its grip. I am still captured by the music of the great River Neva, by the boisterous wind that ruffles the water in the Fontanka Canal and pierces the Summer Garden, and by the dim sunshine that was never enough to warm Klodt's equestrian statues depicting the taming of nature on the Anichkov Bridge.

What better place for me to start with Andrusha on a journey into our past – mine obviously, and his by extension. I did not have far to travel across the Anichkov Bridge, past the columns and Roman warriors, to the Palace of Young Pioneers. I was ten, a girl with excellent marks at school and no idea what to do with herself. I went there with some friends to enrol in a gymnastic group, but I ended up in ballet. I honestly don't remember why.

Before the Revolution the palace belonged to the Queen Mother, Maria Fyodorovna; it was there that the last Russian Tsar, Nicholas II, spent his honeymoon with his young bride. In my time the past was still very much alive – the shiny, waxed parquet floors, the crystal chandeliers and Venetian windows draped with white silk. In accordance with the most popular of all socialist slogans – 'Children Should Get the Best' – the palace was given over to youngsters. Everywhere were swarms of children, playing, singing or dancing. Boys were busy designing and constructing things. When I was young, this was the customary place for the admission ceremony for ten-year-olds into the Young Pioneers; they marched with a red banner and vowed to serve the cause of Marxist-Leninism. I naturally made my vow together with all the rest – there was no other way. I joined the chorus to pledge my dedication to socialism and took my place among the long rows of schoolgirls, all dressed up in starched white aprons, scarlet ties and glistening silk bows. I wonder to what or to whom they now dedicate themselves.

At first I could not grasp quickly enough the choreographic

patterns of the various folk dances, and then a bigger disaster occurred. At a New Year performance I brought confusion into the *corps de ballet* of girls dressed like snowflakes. On stage I not only managed to get my own movements mixed up, but also threw off all the others, so that the entire dance turned into a mess. My teacher suggested that I go to the Vaganova ballet school. 'Things will be more interesting for you there,' she said.

The Vaganova school is situated in one of the most architecturally perfect streets in the world: to walk down Rossi Street makes you aware of balance and harmony. I went there at the age of thirteen and remained at the school for six years before I graduated. The school is named after Agrippina Vaganova, the essential link between the great days of the choreographer Marius Petipa and the teachers of my generation. She died in 1951, but really she is still teaching in the studios – her influence is felt everywhere. Vaganova codified the teaching system which is the basis of our classical technique and style.

And I had an additional reason for showing Andrusha the school. He had organized his classmates in San Francisco to send parcels of vitamins, food and clothing for the children, and he was excited to see some of the recipients for himself.

Has anything much changed in the intervening thirty years? I hear that the school canteen offers better food, for a start. Also there is a new subject in the curriculum – 'The Scriptures'. I meet Father Michael, who tells me that he is reopening the church of Our Lady that was closed down after the Revolution. Well, this is a good intention, though I wonder if it is not more display than commitment. I'm afraid there seems to be a new fashion in Russia that everyone must embrace religion.

The school now boasts a studio which was named in memory of Rudolf Nureyev. It was in this very studio that I saw him for the first time: together with Natalia Dudinskaya he was rehearsing the *pas de deux* from *Giselle*. He was young, with a crop of unruly hair, and to me he looked very strange and wild. Little did I suspect at that time the strange circumstances which would bring us to dance together in so many theatres in the West.

I took Andrusha into the Theatre Museum on the ground floor of the school, and among the numerous exhibits he found a section devoted to my career, replete with photographs spanning many years. This is a great change from the time – it seems only yesterday – when, together with Baryshnikov and Nureyev, all reference to me was locked in the 'classified material department'. Until 1989 every library and museum had one such department, where any mention of my name or of people like me was buried. My photos were destroyed, my films were burned, and according to the *Soviet Encyclopedia of Ballet* I did not exist. Andrusha found it odd, to say the least, that I was once a non-person in the country of my birth. What a paradox that on my last visit to St Petersburg, in 1992 (a mere three years since my reinstatement as a 'person' in this country), the Mayor, Anatoly Sobchak, invited me to stay in the official government residence in Smolny. It was from these very buildings that the 1917 revolutionary leaders directed the course of the armed uprising. Before me, only chosen leaders of the government had stayed there. As a defector, it was unthinkable that I would be so 'honoured'. Times have indeed changed.

After saying farewell to the Vaganova school we walk down Rossi Street to the magnificent Pushkin Drama Theatre (formerly the Alexandrinka). This is a truly extraordinary experience for me. As a child, I used to crane my neck to gaze upon the lofty statue of Apollo and his chariot which crowns the tall columns at the front of the theatre, and dream, as children do, that I might one day be an actress. It is strange to think that years later, in 1992, I did in fact make my dramatic debut here in *Two for the Seesaw*, directed by Roman Viktiuk.

Opposite the theatre lies a little park dominated by a statue of Catherine the Great, where I used to stroll. Now I am told it has become a pleasant rendezvous for the newly emancipated gay men of the city, who somewhat irreverently promise to meet 'at Kate's'.

As Andrusha and I continue our walk along the Nevsky Prospekt we reach the Palace Square, located behind the Winter

Palace that was built in the sublime classical and Russian baroque styles and houses the Hermitage Museum. We come to the canal known as the Zimnyaya Kanavka (the Winter Ditch), a legendary place immortalized by Tchaikovsky in his opera *The Queen of Spades*: Liza, the heroine, drowns herself here after singing her beautiful aria. The famous painter and designer Alexander Benois recreated this symbolic location of old St Petersburg in his scenery for the opera.

I am on my way now to meet Andrei Ananov, one of the most famous Russian jewellers, known in the sparkling capitals of the West as the recognized heir to the traditions and fame of Fabergé. Ananov has not always been where he is now. He is an actor by training, and for many years his activities as a jeweller were illegal. He was persecuted by the KGB, but with the advent of perestroika was permitted to open a shop in the luxurious Europa Hotel. Today, he has a large workshop of forty people who are learning the art of making fine jewellery under him. As a parting present, Ananov gives me a beautiful enamel egg decorated with a gold double-headed imperial eagle. He tells me that he has presented similar eggs to Placido Domingo and Montserrat Caballé.

Ananov and his success are one side of the coin that is called New Russia. There is another side, distressing to behold. I can scarcely believe my eyes when I realize that the long line of people who are hawking wares on the pavement are private citizens selling their possessions in order to live. I cannot get used to the sight of paupers and old-age pensioners in underground passages or hanging around churches, any more than I can find it easy to look tolerantly at kiosks selling a brash variety of foreign wines and spirits. In my time this was called profiteering, but today it is tacitly encouraged. I look into a couple of shops and find shoddy, unfashionable clothes from Taiwan selling at exorbitant prices.

I feel sad for my people. They don't deserve this kind of life. As I walk by the lines of people selling everything imaginable they turn their faces away from embarrassment. I know they have dignity, and they feel they are on the edge of losing it. I can do little here except tread these familiar streets, watching their decline with stricken heart and giving away roubles to numerous beggars who show no enthusiasm. Like everyone else, they prefer dollars.

The St Alexander Nevsky Lavra, the Pantheon of the great and the immortal, is my next call in this long day. I have come here to refresh my spirit after what I have seen – to pay tribute to Marius Petipa, whose great ballet *La Bayadère* I restaged in the West.

Petipa was unique in his understanding of the city's soul and expressed its architecture in his harmonious choreographic patterns. The connection between the two is, I think, indisputable. All the buildings and spatial arrangements in St Petersburg were designed by the best architects in the world – French, Italian, English, German, Dutch – and such a mixture of European cultures exists in this city and nowhere else. In the uniquely Russian fusion of all these styles, space and light were of the utmost significance. The architectural rhythm created by the spacing of windows and columns is reflected in Petipa's geometrically uplifting patterns for the *corps de ballet*. It is no coincidence that he lived here for sixty years.

I cannot leave my city without visiting the theatre which has meant so much in my life, the Maryinsky, home of the Kirov Ballet. It is certainly one of the most beautiful theatres in the world with its magnificent front curtain painted by Golovine, its blue velvet-covered chairs, and the gilded, regal Tsar's box. Not only did I give my first performances here, but when I came home in 1989 I made the decision that it would also be the scene of my last appearance as a classical ballerina. Thus did my career come full circle back to its origins, in a neat sweep of time which gave me tremendous satisfaction. I will never forget that memorable night when I looked up at the Tsar's box and saw my mother and family sitting there after being ostracized for nineteen years. Now, deep in my soul, I want my son to see where I began, and I take him to watch the Kirov perform *La Corsaire*. It is incredibly touching that the audience greets us with warm applause as we take our seats.

Our brief stay in St Petersburg is now over and we prepare to depart on our train journey across Russia and Central Asia. I leave here heavy-hearted but, no matter where my travels take me, St Petersburg will always be, for me, the most beautiful place in the world. I will always feel part of this city. I will always pray for it and love it. Till we meet again.

> Our parting is false:
> you and I are inseparable.
> My shadow is on your walls,
> my reflection in the canals.
> *Anna Akhmatova*

It's not that I don't like trains, but my hectic international lifestyle never allowed me enough time to enjoy them. What I didn't like was the pre-departure chaos. When I was a child, we went by train to the Baltic for our summer holidays, loaded down with food for the family. I remember vividly my slenderly built, small stepfather carrying an enormous suitcase on his head while my mother, carrying my little stepbrother in her arms, and I elbowed our way through the dense crowd trying to keep up with him. While I was standing on the platform I would look forward to climbing up on to the upper berth in our train compartment, where I would nibble a cracker and watch the scenery slide by.

Trains in Russian classical literature always seem to signify misfortune, a threatening force which, like fate, closes in on you with its irrefutable power. Just think of Tolstoy's Anna Karenina, that image of a woman standing on the rails. I am not standing on the rails; I am in a comfortable coupé of a luxury train called Rus (the Bolshoi Express) on my way to Moscow, our first stop.

This train was built in Russian workshops in the early 1950s and restored to its present impressive standard in the 1990s. The vintage coaches were originally intended for use by government officials. The new business men of the Ministry of Railways now recognize the potential commercial value of such tourist trains and a new joint venture called Inter-Track has been established with the UK-based Cox & Kings, a partnership which has enabled them to refurbish the train and set this enterprise in motion. We are told that on certain stretches of the track the carriages will be coupled to historic steam locomotives which we will have a chance to see up close.

Moscow

For a long time it seemed that Moscow was the only city that mattered in my country. Others, including my beloved St Petersburg/Leningrad, comprised the back yard. It wasn't just arrogant Muscovites who held this attitude. Across the entire former Soviet Union, people were convinced that if you wanted to establish a career or live the good life you had to go to Moscow. The Central Government was there, as was the omnipotent Ministry of Culture, the place where official gala concerts were held that could seal your fate as a performer. Even for us ballet artistes, the Bolshoi Theatre stood first and foremost as the symbol of statehood. Everyone wanted to go to the Bolshoi because it was easier to make a career there, to be noticed and perhaps to receive coveted awards such as People's Artist or the Lenin Prize. Unfortunately, from the 1930s many of our great artistes abandoned Leningrad to go to the Bolshoi, among them Semenova, Ulanova and even the present Director of the Bolshoi, Yuri Grigorovich. At one time I was toying with the idea myself, but in the end I decided I had to take more radical steps to extend my artistic horizons.

I doubt if I would have enjoyed living in Moscow. After St Petersburg, with its beauty and harmony, I couldn't succumb to Moscow's charm. Somehow the hustle and bustle of the place just didn't appeal to me. But, of course, it did have its own specific kind of appeal, its own frenetic rhythm. People always seemed to conduct themselves more freely in Moscow. There was always more sunshine in this city. It was always full of tourists speaking all kinds of foreign languages. You would only have to walk along Gorky Street (now its old name, Tverskaya, has been restored) to feel the intense pulse of the capital, the noisy crowds, the abundance of official black limousines. This irrepressible flow of people hurrying down the street always made me feel on my guard and kept me constantly looking over my shoulder so as not to be run over by these teeming masses. This is the Moscow I remember, and it seems unchanged.

For me the most impressive sight in Moscow, and still the pre-eminent tourist haunt, is the Kremlin with its massive red-brick walls, the gilt cupola of Ivan Veliky, the glass cube of the Palace of Congresses, the multi-coloured onion domes of St Basil's Cathedral, and of course Lenin's tomb. Where else can you find a deceased leader embalmed and exhibited for over sixty years? There is a research institute whose sole duty is to maintain Lenin's body in presentable condition – such a morbid, weird idea. Yet I remember how shocked I first was when it was decided that, in accordance with his dying wish, Lenin's body would be removed to the Volkov cemetery in Leningrad. But after thinking about it, it seemed to me quite natural and appropriate. I was surprised when a storm of public protest erupted; elderly people marched alongside the obvious staunch Communists and, to my amazement, so did young people – all proclaiming their dismay with banners displaying the slogan: 'Hands off Lenin.' The powers that be wisely decided to uphold the status quo; Lenin remained, and the hourly changing of the guard continued. I remember the long queues of people waiting for hours, as I did myself years ago, to see Lenin, the man responsible for the 'happiness' of the past seventy years and the terrible confusion of today. As I stand and look out over Red Square today, with my son, it seems empty and deserted. No one is waiting to see Lenin now. Nevertheless it may take years before this, the Red Square branch of Madame Tussaud's, will be shut for ever.

In the same vein, our next stop is what I would call the

graveyard of monuments. In Moscow, there were more monuments and statues honouring the Communist Party and outstanding state leaders than anywhere else. Some were quite good; I mean the monuments, of course, not the leaders. In August 1991 they were swept off their granite pedestals by a 'wave of popular fury'. Felix Dzerzhinsky, known as 'Iron Felix', the founding father of the KGB, was the first and natural victim. Today, he has been supplanted by a wooden cross in memory of the Gulag inmates; together with his cronies he has been banished to a green lawn outside the House of Artists. What a sight is this graveyard of fallen idols. A marble Stalin lies on the ground with his nose knocked off and his feet a little distance away, still attached to their pedestal. He looks somewhat contemplative, lying there comfortably amid the ruins. Behind him Kalinin looms, spotted all over with bird droppings, and a huge Sverdlov stands holding a bronze folder. I wonder what he had kept in it? Were there ciphered telegrams about the horrible fate of the Tsar and his family, or lists of executed hostages, or plans for the programmes to do away with the intellectuals and peasants? Much has now been published, but even more remains concealed. It is somehow sinister to see these statues discarded here; perhaps they should have been left in place to remind people of these men's evil deeds.

Moscow reminds me of New York in that I feel pressed for time here – the tempo of life is accelerated. So we quickly move on to a circus school where students practise in a replica big top. They, like so many other aspiring professionals, are no longer guaranteed jobs after they graduate. This school, which is unique, used to supply the world-famous Moscow State Circus, but may now have to close due to lack of funds. The changes in this new Russia include privatization of circuses, which are going out of business because the animals are too expensive to feed. The trained animals are given to the zoos.

As we enter the arena we are surrounded by talented young students, each practising their particular trick with their individual coach. There are acrobats, jugglers and trapeze artistes, all working simultaneously in their own corner of the ring. Andru-sha goes off to get a closer look while I talk to the director of the school, Victor Vladimirov, who graduated from here in 1954 and then became a performer. He adamantly assures me that, despite their present difficulties and no matter what government is in power, the circus will never die. He says, 'The circus enjoys great popularity, not only here, but all over the world. It appeals to something fundamental in human nature, which is to worship the spirit of human strength where man himself is God.' He explains that Russia is at heart a pagan nation, used to admiring humans who can do extraordinary feats rather than deities for whom miracles are easy. For this reason the circus became a genuine art form and circus performers have always been looked up to – even when the Church tried to forbid it. He goes on, 'The performer is forced and bound to overcome grave difficulties and emerge the victor from the most dangerous and complicated situations. That's what we teach our students.'

Concerning the state of Russia now, he says, 'Perestroika has complicated our lives but it is just a temporary phenomenon.' He makes it clear that he hopes things will revert to a form of Communism. I realize that he was a hard-line Communist who, out of necessity, adapted himself to his new environment to retain his position. His words weigh heavily on me. I well remember this type of overbearing, authoritarian figure. An aggressive man who pushes aside the opinions of others and listens only to himself, he proceeds to lecture me about the arts, specifically ballet and theatre. 'Any creative work on stage is all lies. The circus is the only exception. Trained muscles and head-spinning acrobatics performed high above the arena without a net, that is true art. It is the art that tells no lies, that issues no calls, that flatters no one and tempts no one. The art that worships the trained body rather than illusion and imagery. The spirit is superfluous; it is the body that matters.'

It is pointless and unnecessary to defend my art. He is holding forth like a programmed automaton, and the small acrobats in the arena begin to look like automatons too. Many of them will go through life with the one stunt they learned in school, which they will repeat over and over until they retire or an injury cuts short their career. Nearly all these children come from poor and unhappy families, and the circus is their only chance in life — hence their absolute devotion to their 'art' and their dictatorial director.

Our next stop, another non-tourist attraction, is even more off the beaten track but is interesting for me. It is the workshop of the Bolshoi Theatre, where the most important element in the life of a ballerina is made — the pointe shoe. The three women I am visiting here have each spent forty-five years of their lives making shoes for the company's leading ballerinas. Each pointe shoe is still made by hand — a long and laborious process; they are very proud of the work they do, and rightly so. They have made shoes for several generations of great ballerinas including Semenova, Ulanova, Plisetskaya and Maximova. Now their workshop has become part of another new joint venture in Russia, backed by Swiss and German investors, and their shoes are sold all over the world. Abroad, they cost as much as $45 a pair, whereas in Russia they are still sold for about 1000 roubles. But some things don't seem to change. For their efforts and skill these women still receive a pittance, as all the money goes to the joint venture and probably the Bolshoi itself. But they don't complain. They accept life as it is.

I try on a pair of shoes, to find that they are indeed comfortable. I tell the women what difficulties I have had over the years in the West to get shoes created for me according to my needs. They must not only be comfortable, but have a good shape, the necessary support — and especially they must be noiseless. I hate it most of all when a ballerina has noisy shoes. To solve that problem, I used to break in my shoes by putting them in a door hinge, and I ruined many doors in theatres throughout the world. Finally, at the end of my ballet career, I received the ideal shoes. But I don't dance any more, and now I have boxes of them lying at home.

Even though my schedule in Moscow is very tight, I can't

leave here without talking to my favourite theatre director, Roman Viktiuk, with whom I worked in *Two for the Seesaw*. Viktiuk's fame and popularity in Moscow, and throughout Russia for that matter, are based not only on his great talent but also on his belief in his inalienable right to stage any play on any theme regardless of what the authorities dictate. He has taken that freedom of expression to the limit, and took risks with dangerous themes at a time when such temerity always met with severe punishment. His all-male production of Genet's *The Maids* in 1988 caused a furore with the censors, but he defied them all. Homosexuality was then against the law, punishable by imprisonment, and it is only recently that the law has been repealed. To stage a play on a homosexual theme was unheard of. His next production, *M. Butterfly*, met similar protests from the authorities but he continued to ignore them.

Viktiuk's position is clear. He says: 'The state has no right to interfere with a person's freedom to love. Lovers are the enemies of the state, in the highest sense of the word, because they challenge society by demonstrating their freedom from its control. Any manifestation of love must aggravate the totalitarian state; it is a fundamental assertion of independence against the world of the absurd.'

Roman described the artistic and moral implications of this view – that if expression of love is forbidden, then it must be embraced and trumpeted by artistic means.

'How can you have forbidden themes in art?' I ask.

Roman answers, 'Art must always breathe the air of freedom, so that the oppressed may look to it for release. That is why *The Maids* is so popular; it refreshes where the state smothers, it celebrates what the state for so long humiliated – the dignity of the individual human being.' I saw that Roman's assault against philistinism had a wider dimension; he recognized, in fact, the responsibility of the theatre to acknowledge and discuss matters otherwise ignored.

To me, it is regrettable only that his production of *The Maids* should end with a display of near-naked men cavorting across the boards, which has nothing to do with Genet's text. I think this kind of display is more appropriate in a nightclub than as the climax to such a serious play. Roman justifies this scene by saying he wanted to suggest that the supremacy and joy of love triumph over whatever barriers society may impose. 'It is the moment the audience has waited for, as they have never seen anything so unconventionally jubilant before.'

I could not help thinking it a pity that Russia takes not only the best of Western ideas, but also the worst – the cheap and tawdry ones, including prostitution and striptease. Pornography is pouring into Russia. Roman's response is: 'It's natural, considering that we never had any sort of sex education. We were always told that there was no such thing as prostitution. It was unthinkable that a Soviet woman could give herself in return for money to a man. And so, of course, now, when everything has been opened up, this has all come out in perverted and excessive form. We need to appeal to the best, the highest things in man. But imagine, for example, the sea and a wave. There are all sorts of horrible things floating about on the surface, but down below everything is clean and there are fish living. So a wave has just broken over us. We have grabbed the surface refuse and haven't looked beneath the wave. Now we must dive down, and this is the process which we are trying to further. But it will take time.'

Andrusha's reaction to our conversation was shock that it should take courage to discuss homosexual themes in the first place, even more that there should be no sex education in Russia and that married couples scarcely talk about sex at all. Brought up in the West, he takes the right to information for granted, and cannot conceive of sexual expression being a subject for punishment.

Time to move on. Roman has to go to a rehearsal and I want to make my last stop at the Novodevichy monastery.

As I arrive at Novodevichy church, I see women gathering outside the church around long wooden tables. These Russian Orthodox believers have come to have their Easter food blessed by the priest. They place their home-made *kulich* (Russian Easter bread) with a candle in it, *paskha* (a rich mixture of sweetened curds with raisins) and coloured Easter eggs on the tables. I quickly find a nearby bakery and buy a *kulich* to enable me to join the group. I place it, along with Ananov's enamel egg and my two crosses, on the table with the other colourfully displayed food.

The priest is a young man in a black cassock with a gold cross. He approaches the table, looking at me intently, and asks me where I am from. I tell him I am Russian Orthodox and live far away in America. 'My name is Natalia Makarova and I am a ballerina.' He smiles warmly and says, 'I thought so, but I couldn't believe my eyes that you are really here.' He takes my crosses into the church to say a special blessing alone. When he returns, he presents me with a wooden egg beautifully painted with an image of Novodevichy church and says, 'God bless you and your family.' I am deeply touched by his attention and genuine interest in me.

Nowhere else is my feeling of belonging to Russia as acute as in an Orthodox church looking at the sorrowful faces of the saints gazing from golden icons. I treasure this special moment of being alone with my Motherland, my past and the saints who have watched over me throughout these years. I pray for the future of my people, for them to find the strength to overcome such difficult times, and I leave the monastery with an enlightened feeling of peace.

Volgograd and the Mamaev Kurgan

Volgograd, formerly called Stalingrad, is approached through the beautiful foothills of the Zhiguli and Hawk Mountains. It is the largest port on the River Volga, and its economic and strategic importance made it a natural target for the Nazis during the Second World War.

Looking out of the train, I see a clean-swept, sleepy, boring city with low houses and wide squares. The inevitable socialist tags in street names, such as Lenin Prospekt and Komsomol Street, are still everywhere, but old slogans such as 'Labour Enriches Our Lives' are now paradoxically juxtaposed with billboards proclaiming 'Volgograd Is for Privatization' and 'Dental Services for the Rich'. During the war, 75 per cent of the city was destroyed. It was built anew in the fifties, which accounts for the colossal, unexciting, Stalinist architectural style. Symbols of the deceased Soviet Union, the hammer and sickle, are still there, as is the inevitable Lenin statue in the central square.

Rita, our guide, tells us how the city suffers from extreme climatic conditions – droughts in summer and acute frosts in winter. But worst of all is the effect of the oil-processing plant which produces something called *baduzin*, a poisonous chemical waste that pollutes both the air and the water of the Volga. During the seventy years of Soviet power this great river became a sewer, and the people are suffocating from the poisonous smog. All efforts by both public and authorities to remedy the situation are more or less in vain.

We go straight to the most important place in Volgograd – the Mamaev Kurgan, a grandiose memorial complex dedicated to all those who defended the wartime city. This complex of monumental architecture and statuary evokes an atmosphere of tragic and sombre beauty. Crowning the ensemble a vast figure of Mother Russia rises nearly 280 feet (85 metres) into the air. She stands wind-blown and indomitable, brandishing a sword in her hand. Uninhibited by its 8000 tons (8,128,400 kg) of weight, the statue seems to soar, to embody and embrace the everlasting memory of those who died defending Stalingrad. This is the impressive symbol of a great victory. You can't take your eyes off it – its power is mesmerizing.

People need this monument. Those who have lived through the war come here on Victory Day to honour the memory of their fallen comrades-in-arms. Young people come here to ascend the long stairway of two hundred steps, one for each day of the unprecedented, heroic and bloody battle for Stalingrad.

I am particularly moved by the circular memorial hall where the expressive, Rodin-like shaped hand holds a burning torch. This eternal flame mournfully reflects and flickers off the surrounding walls. Here the endless list of names of the fallen are engraved in gold. All of them, soldiers and officers alike, died here in obedience to the order: 'Not one step back.' May their memory live for ever.

My father might be among them. I have no recollection of him. I was a few months old when the war started and he left for the front. He disappeared without a trace. My grandfather, his father, died in the 900-day siege of Leningrad and my grandmother, unable to cope with the hardship, hanged herself.

As I read the names of the dead on the tablets, I come face-to-face with history, with all the suffering, grief and lost lives reflected in the eternal flame. For me they are not just names on an endless list, but rather living images. And above all this rises the sublime music of Schumann, a German, ascending towards the sky enveloping our sorrow, love and lasting memory of the fallen.

Volgograd is a Cossack city and great pains were taken to arrange a festival especially for our film. We were promised hundreds of horsemen, singing and dancing with sabres. It was all carefully planned to take place on Easter Day. It seemed quite strange to me that these festivities were scheduled to take place on such a religious holiday, but I was assured that it was all confirmed: 'Cossacks always keep their word!' When the time came, one lonely, elderly Cossack with a long white beard arrived on horseback to inform us that no one was going to show up. He was at a loss to explain what had happened to the others; they had just all disappeared. I felt sorry for him. He was obviously the unlucky one sent to break the bad news. The best laid plans . . .

But, as far as I was concerned, all was not lost. I had a chance to attend Easter midnight service, which is always such a special occasion for me and which I longed to attend in the new Russia. I found a different atmosphere from what I had expected owing

1. (*Left*) Mark Tully crossing the Ayub Bridge on an inspector's trolley.

2. (*Below*) The badge of Pakistan Railways.

3. (*Bottom*) Steam trains at Jacobabad Junction.

4. A train crossing a bridge near Rawalpindi.

5. The special steam train from Peshawar puffing through the mountains on its way to the Khyber Pass.

6. An aerial view of the passenger train between Campo Grande and Miranda crossing the flood plains of the Pantanal.

7. (*Main picture*) Sunset on the Pantanal.
8. (*Inset*) A jabiru stork, the symbol of the Pantanal.

9. Dawn over a village near Miranda in the Pantanal swamp.

10. A 'Metropolitan Line' train on the Kowloon–Canton service.

11, 12. (*Top and bottom left*) Trains at the main railway station in Shanghai,
including a double-decker.
13. (*Bottom right*) At weekends old men take their pet birds to Beijing's parks and squares
for some fresh air.

14. Traditional tents, or gers, together with ordinary housing, on the outskirts of Ulaan Baatar.

15, 16, 17. The Bolshoi Express, the train on which Makarova travelled from St Petersburg to Tashkent in Uzbekistan.

18. Samarkand: the Tillya-Kari madrassah in Registan.

19. (*Left*) Michael Palin with Lord O'Neill on the private railway that runs through his estate at Shanes Castle, on the shores of Lough Neagh.

20, 21. (*Bottom left and right*) Evidence of loving care and long hours of spit and polish on a Shanes Castle locomotive.

22. (*Left*) The Tralee and Dingle Light Railway to Blennerville.

23. (*Bottom*) The City Gold speeds through countryside near Buttevant in Co. Cork.

24, 25, 26. (*Opposite, left and bottom*) The Banana Express near Port Shepstone in southern Natal.

27. The steam engine of the North East Cape Rail company, with its one carriage, in the foothills of the Drakensberg Mountains, near Barkly East.

to the presence of young teenagers, about Andrusha's age, pushing their way through the crowd towards the altar. The girls
were heavily made up and wore short skirts, while the boys had
the latest haircuts but were quite dishevelled-looking. As they
held their candles they loudly discussed their own teenage problems, completely disrupting the solemnity of the occasion; the
elderly people clung to the walls to keep out of their way, afraid
of being crushed. These young people seemed to be in church
not because they had embraced religion, but merely for the sake
of appearance. It was as if they were treating religion as a kind of
insurance policy for the future. I have noticed that this new
surge of religion in Russia seems to be a shallow, ritualistic
exercise without any spiritual depth or commitment. Being
christened is now fashionable. I hope I am wrong, for it is
encouraging to see young people make the choice to attend
church rather than a disco.

In my time, the idea of going to church would never have
entered our heads. During the Soviet regime we were brought
up in the atheistic tradition, based on Lenin's belief that 'Religion
is the opium of the masses'. Only our grandmothers (*babushkas*)
would dare to go. My grandmother had me secretly christened
when I was five years old; this was not easy, since so many
churches were closed, used for storage or destroyed. As shocking
as it seems, I have been told that some of the clergy were on the
payroll of the KGB. Apparently each had his secret codename,
and their duties were to report the secrets of the confessional to
the state. People suffered dreadfully as a result. It seems that
some members of this same clergy are still at the helm of the
Orthodox Church. Today, it is said that 'Yesterday's KGB
agents are today's Church leaders, just as yesterday's hard-line
Communists are today's Democrats'. However, the new generation of priests, I am told, have changed for the better. They
want to propagate the teachings of the Church and her faith. A
devout believer said to me, 'Communism raped the Church and
raped the country for seventy-five years.' It will take at least a
generation for the wounds to heal. Today's generation of newly

baptized Orthodox faithful seem to be like lost children in the forest; I hope they find their way.

Astrakhan

Finally we arrive in the caviar centre of the world (Hoorah!), hoping to catch our own Beluga and eat the caviar on the spot, a treat which of course would be the highlight of our film. No, no, no . . . It is not as simple as we think (or hope).

Astrakhan lies on the delta where the great Volga flows into the Caspian Sea. Until three years ago it was closed to foreigners owing to the presence of a nearby cosmodrome. The city was an important trading point on the old Silk Route; merchants' houses line the canal and signs of different ethnic groups are everywhere. In the old town, picturesque low wooden houses decay and collapse into rubbish-strewn streets. By the river, broad promenades are served by intricately-carved landing stages and in spring the local men sit outside and eat *vobla*, small dried river fish, and wash them down with bottles of beer. I remember the taste of this salty fish from my childhood, but without the beer.

We set off to find our Beluga, which involves an endless drive along dusty roads miles away from Astrakhan. Eventually we arrive at Lenin's Way, a sturgeon fishery. This is a world of sweltering heat so intense that it immobilizes the Volga, drives dogs into the shade and scorches fishermen's faces. Amid their nets, spread out to dry in the sun, the fishermen watch us dispassionately as we unload our cameras and other paraphernalia. Dressed in bright orange waterproofs and thigh-high rubber boots, they are all Kazaks, oriental-looking with high, wide cheekbones, ruddy faces and black, black eyes. They speak among themselves in their own language. When I walk over to talk to them they answer my questions in broken Russian. They tell me that the Volga hydroelectric power station has destroyed 90 per cent of the river's sturgeon, that what caviar there is is mostly exported, and that the local people have to buy fish and caviar from poachers. The fishermen's work is hard and tedious and decidedly unglamorous. Try standing in the water for five hours or more and you won't want any caviar either. Nothing has changed as a result of Gorbachev's perestroika; the collective farm is now called a 'partnership', but the same bosses remain. Even the name of this collective fish farm, Lenin's Way, has not been changed. They say there is no point in changing it. Lenin is still a household name in Russia.

We stand around watching the fishermen work. It is a slow laborious process which takes about an hour and a half. First the enormous net is taken out by motorboat and spread over a large area of water. Then the fishermen who remain on the shore walk slowly along, dragging the net and pulling it gradually landwards. We anxiously await the results of the catch. The net is full of small, wriggling fish which the fishermen playfully start throwing to Andrusha and me. They are slippery and jump out of our hands. What fun! 'Mom, look at that one,' Andrusha exclaims, pointing to a fish a metre long, jumping up and down in the net. Bravo, success – caviar! The fishermen look at us with ironical expressions as if to say, 'You fools, can't you see it's a baby sturgeon?' – no caviar. All our enthusiasm is in vain. How are we supposed to know? It looks mature to us. They explain that Ocetra, the smaller kind of sturgeon, carries caviar for about ten years. If it escapes being caught, it can live up to fifteen or even twenty years.

Hours go by with little action as the net is spread again, and we are about to give up hope that any adult sturgeon will be caught. The crew is beginning to pack up the gear when suddenly we see the fishermen rushing through the water, pulling the net over to a boat close to the shore. As we get closer, Andrusha screams, 'Oh my God, Mom, it's a shark!' But in fact, there in the net is an enormous Beluga, the largest kind of sturgeon. Andrusha and I jokingly agree it looks longer than Dad if he were lying down in the water. The fishermen estimate it weighs 350 lb (160 kg). They put a large, thick rope through its fin and out of its mouth like a noose and tie it to the end of the boat. Then they slowly pull it to the shore. One of the fishermen sits on top of it, patting its glistening white sides.

We anxiously wait for them to cut it open, but we are told that this will be impossible. It is a criminal offence – all fish must go to the Kirov fish cannery where the caviar is processed. They placate us by telling us that the unprocessed caviar is actually tasteless, although very good for you. We must believe them. But our curiosity is piqued and we try to negotiate a deal. We offer them dollars. No one will know, we assure them. They are tempted, but decide it's not worth the risk of imprisonment. Disappointed, we say our goodbyes and start the long drive back to Astrakhan, empty-handed and hungry.

My next assignment is a secret meeting with a fish poacher, called *brakaniery*. We drive to a remote place, pick up an unidentified man at a prearranged location and then proceed to an even more obscure place for this top-secret interview. He is taking a big risk in talking to me for the film. He begins by telling me that there is no caviar for sale in Astrakhan and how important poachers are to the local economy.

'We feed the people. Without us they would starve. We are not thieves – the government is. The fishermen are obliged to turn over whatever they catch to the government-controlled canneries, and everything is exported. In the fifties and sixties no one counted fish. There was enough for everyone and, if you kept some, the authorities would look the other way. The law was rarely enforced. Then the dam was built and the streams feeding the river dried up. This dam hurt the fishing industry, but it took a long time for the local authorities to fully realize the problem they had created. They then had to find a way of letting the fish through, but fish had already become scarce and fishermen could no longer get away with keeping any of their catch. Out of necessity I started poaching fish, and there are many others like me. We lead a dangerous existence, because if we're caught we can be imprisoned for up to eight years. My friend was caught yesterday – he got five years. The state is wrong to deprive us of food at a time when it is scarce.'

'If you end up in jail, what will you do then?' I ask.

'When I get out, I will poach again. After all, I have a family – my wife and three daughters – to feed. It is my responsibility to take care of them.'

I wish him well and thank him for his candidness.

Back in Astrakhan, we ride through the old town with its colourful, low wooden houses adorned with amazingly intricate, lace-like fretwork. I take a walk along the streets to get a closer look at these miniature dwellings with their slanted roofs. At one time they must have been charming; now they look run-down with their peeling paint and broken fences. I catch myself looking into the windows, peeping through the potted geraniums which decorate the sills, trying to catch a glimpse inside. I try to guess what kind of life goes on behind the lace curtains.

I must look somewhat out of place on these streets. I attract attention from passers-by and am approached by a man who anxiously wants to talk to me. To his delight, he discovers I speak Russian and he pulls me towards his dilapidated house – for vodka, he says. I ask how he makes a living. He answers simply and directly: 'I am a thief.'

'Ah,' I reply, with my expression unchanged.

From another gate a man rushes over to us, yelling, 'Please come and look. I must show you how we live. Maybe someone will listen.' I leave the thief behind, promising to return, and follow my new guide.

Oh, my God – what a sight lies before me. His house is completely submerged in water. When he opens the high fence leading to what should be his yard, I see water lying level with the door. A wooden walkway over the water is the only way to cross to the hut outside where the toilet is located. Next to this stands a neighbour's identical hut. The water is full of refuse and sewage. I have never seen such deplorable conditions. I can't hold back my tears. How can people be forced to live this way?

I ask him, 'Why has nothing been done to help you?'

He replies, 'We have gone to the local authorities but nothing happens, and we have been living this way for five years.'

His wife and beautiful seventeen-year-old daughter join us on the walkway. The daughter dreams of going to the West. Who can blame her?

Neighbours gather around, shouting at me to come and look at their homes. They are in the same condition, with water knee-high. They complain that some of the children have tuberculosis, while others are susceptible to various diseases as a result of the insanitary conditions. An old woman tells me she has to go to bed each night in her coat and boots. They ask me to let people know how they live, and look at me with hope in their eyes. How I wish there could be some way to help these people. Five years of perestroika have done nothing to improve their lives.

On the Rus Train

Our steam train is like a snorting steel stallion of superlative power and beauty which the wind cannot catch as it thunders across the steppe. Outside the train stretches a boundless desert, while inside its cosy compartments furnished with velvet-covered armchairs, towelling bathrobes and complimentary cosmetics make life pleasant. Three restaurants (Georgian, Ukrainian and Baltic), staffed with perfectly trained and exquisitely polite waiters, confound the imagination. In Russia service and a smile do not usually go together; a simple 'thank you' from a waiter is so rare it sounds like music to the ears. In restaurants you have to be prepared to wait, to ignore bad manners and even worse service. I rarely went to restaurants in the Soviet Union.

Here, on the train, I am proud to say that both service and food are up to international standards. I try not to think that it might have to do with the hard currencies the tourists are paying to the railway company. Each carriage has two attendants, called *provodnitsy*. Olga and Lena, the two nice girls who are looking after us, are always ready to fulfil any request. When we return, half dead after long hours of filming, they greet us with warmth and concern. They make our train a delightful home from home.

The person I am most impressed by on this trip is also named Olga. Olga Zvorykina works for an organization called Travel Russia and is in charge of co-ordinating this trip and our complicated filming schedule. She is truly amazing – a lovely young woman, probably in her early twenties, charming, trust-worthy and competent. I would hope that she is typical of her generation of capable young people who are working hard at their profession. If she can organize things to run so smoothly here in this chaotic time in Russia, then she can succeed any-where. Whoever makes this journey through Russia will be lucky if they have Olga to take care of them.

Gradually I begin to love the constant motion of the train. I wake up in the mornings with my muscles feeling relaxed as if I have had a good massage. My usual stiff back feels supple and flexible. My daily routine of exercises is necessary no matter where I am – it does not change just because I am on a train. I find a way to adapt to my constrained surroundings. Putting my leg on the upper berth is perfect for my stretches. To limber up my muscles, I sit on the lower berth with my legs stretched in a split, with one foot touching one wall while the other foot touches the opposite wall. The passageway is also a good place for my exercises. The bar across the window is the right height to use as a ballet barre. By slightly opening the top window I can stretch further by lifting my leg and placing it on the rim. I surprise more than one passenger as they try to get by to their compartments, but I just push my leg higher up the wall, flattening my body to an angle of 180 degrees, to let them pass. By their expressions I see how weird I must look.

The biggest excitement for all of us, passengers and film crew alike, is the steam engine which is attached to our train for parts of this trip. I am filmed and photographed climbing all over this massive machine (each wheel is as tall as myself!) while rising steam envelops me. I feel at home in this cloud-like atmosphere, which is an effect commonly used in *Swan Lake, Giselle, La Bayadère* and other romantic ballets. The clouds represented my descending into the grave or ascending into another world – the only problem was that my toe shoes would inevitably get wet and ruined, but it was usually the end of the ballet anyway and the curtain would come down. However on this occasion, as I am climbing on to the front of the engine, I am wearing high waterproof boots and the curtain doesn't come down. Instead, we go full speed ahead . . . *en avant* . . .

The demanding filming schedule keeps me away from my fellow travellers who congregate in the bar every evening. My son, delighted with his newly found 'adult' freedom, frequents it for the two of us. 'What do you do there?' I ask him one morning when he nearly misses breakfast and another day of filming.

'I communicate,' comes his succinct reply.

I find it hard to communicate with him, at least recently. He obviously likes being filmed but is embarrassed, if not displeased, to pose with me in front of the camera.

I try to find out what Andrusha has liked and disliked so far on this trip and what he thought of Russia. 'Well,' he replies, 'the real Russia is a far cry from what tourist guides would have you believe. Balalaikas and *matreshka* dolls are for the tourists – they don't represent the genuine Russia. They are just kitsch to be sold on the Arbat together with cans of caviar past their sell-by date. For me, Russia is a gloomy stream of people all dressed alike in dark coats, trudging along through muddy streets oblivious to their surroundings. Why do they find it hard to smile? I suppose they are poor and can't afford good food, and the climate is not the best. Can you imagine living with snow and rain falling on you for six months of the year, turning everything to mud? And look at the endless lines of people waiting to buy food or essentials! I don't suppose you would smile after spending hours and hours in them. Well, poverty can't be the only reason for their gloom. Here in Asia, people seem much more cordial; they smile and talk to us, and do some folk dancing to honour us. Yet they seem to be no richer than the Russians.'

'Probably it's because the climate is better,' I comment, making a feeble attempt to answer. I feel that I cannot explain anything to him, a boy born in a different country and practically a different civilization. He has learnt about Russia from my chaotic descriptions, American tourist guides and geography lessons. For him this country remains an undiscovered, enigmatic continent, the mysterious land where his somewhat eccentric mother was born.

Asia: Khiva, Bukhara and Samarkand

Asia, with its scorching hot wind and burning sand, smothers us with its heat. Andrusha was right: Asia is different. It is looking at us with its attentive, lynx, oriental eyes. I have never been here before, though I have heard and read about its famed beauty – a beauty that captures your soul.

Khiva, Bukhara and Samarkand, the most fascinating cities in Uzbekistan, live in the desert's hot embrace. In summer temperatures rise to 112°F (50°C) in the shade, and there are no tours and no tourists. The country comes to life in the cooler spring and autumn weather. Each of the three cities is ingeniously constructed in a circular layout which always leaves one side of the street in the shade. The upward perspective is dominated by the imposing sky-blue domes and tall, slender minarets of mosques, which hang like a mirage above the sun-baked houses. Here life itself seems like a mirage, whether I am crossing the threshold of cool tombs or enjoying the rippling, streaming water of the *aryks* (streams) or hiding myself in the shade of magnificent acacias and wide, spreading elms. These trees were planted here God knows when, and have witnessed the passing of aeons of time and countless events. I wonder, has the life lived under the shady branches disappeared or changed beyond recognition, leaving behind only the ruins and pavements overgrown with grass?

The Great Silk Route, along which trade caravans made their way from China and India to the interior of Asia, ran through these cities. In the fourteenth century Tamerlane, a fierce military leader and eminent statesman, founded his mighty empire and made Samarkand its capital. He intended it to eclipse, in luxury and beauty, all the other cities of the orient. Here lived great thinkers and philosophers of the East, such as Abn Sina and Al Horazmi. The palaces, mosques and madrassahs (Islamic seminaries) were the centres of intense cultural and intellectual life. Much of this has been lost, never to be revived; Asian people paid a high price for the centuries of first Tsarist and then Soviet domination. Yet the spirit and captivating mystery of the ancient Uzbek cities survive.

Khiva, a city constructed from dazzling white stone, was the capital of Kwarazm in the first century BC. Now it is like a ghost city. As the ancient trading centre of the Kara Kum Desert, it is the least-known of the historic Uzbek cities. The inner city of Ishan-Kala is now a 'museum city', a maze of mosques, madrassahs, caravanserais (traders' inns), bath-houses and harems. Treading its streets, I feel as if I am walking through the set for a film of the *Arabian Nights*. In fact, it seems I am. Our guide tells us that an American film company was here recently, shooting *Ali Baba and His Forty Thieves*. This city seems as silent and bereft as if Genghis Khan had just left, his famous hordes replaced with groups of tourists wandering along the narrow streets and souvenir sellers calling out lazily from the shade.

The most impressive monument in Khiva is the mausoleum of Pakhlavan Mahmud. According to a legend dating from the fourteenth century, Mahmud was a tanner turned poet-philosopher who gave away all his money to the poor. One of his many verses decorating the tiled walls reads: 'It is better to live a hundred years in prison than talk for one minute to a fool.' I don't agree!

The Khan's palace, another important edifice, is not as sumptuous as one would expect. Despite its dazzling tiled walls, it is somewhat austere and has a mysterious and strangely nostalgic air. The three colours used in the tilework are traditional – white for water, blue for the sky and green for nature; these combinations are seen everywhere, on clay souvenir dishes as well as the seventeenth-century tiles adorning the madrassah walls. Their beauty calms the soul and infuses it with tranquillity, purity and freshness.

In the Khan's harem, we see a huge wooden bed designed for his favourite wife. He could have up to four official wives whom he had to support; the rest (sometimes as many as forty!) had to support themselves with sewing and embroidery, never leaving the small courtyard of the harem. Each of them lived under the threat of 'Talik'. This word, if uttered once by the Khan, was a warning. Repeated three times it meant an instant divorce, and an order to leave the harem immediately. The wives had nothing they could call their own except the clothes on their backs, so the most resourceful of them refused to be parted from their jewellery, which could weigh up to 45 lb (20 kg). Even at night they wore it, always prepared for a sudden eviction; that jewellery was an insurance policy against poverty.

Back on the train, we travel all evening and through the night to reach Bukhara. This city's great days began in the ninth and tenth centuries, when it was the seat of the Samanid dynasty. Even after their fall, it remained an intellectual and commercial centre. Bukhara continued to flourish whenever Samarkand was in decline, and vice versa – except when they were both devastated by Genghis Khan. An oasis town, it took seven days by camel to get to Samarkand.

Bukhara was known in the medieval Muslim East as the 'noble and glorious stronghold of the faith', and it is here that we begin to become aware of the recent resurgence of Islam. The beautiful ancient mosques and madrassahs with their restrained decoration are once again filled with eager worshippers and students. The Kukeldash madrassah, built in 1558–69, is the largest still standing in Central Asia.

The liberation movement of 1927 emancipated women in Central Asia. They could abandon their yashmaks or veils, receive a proper education and learn men's trades. We went to see women working at the gold embroidery factory, which before that revolution was a privileged occupation only for men. The thread contains 10 per cent gold, and until the 1930s women were not allowed to sew with it as it was commonly believed that a woman's touch deprived gold of its glint. Now I see hundreds of women gathered together in a huge, stuffy workshop embroidering skull caps, traditional robes and slippers under the careful supervision of the shop master. They are paid by the piece. Strange as it may seem, most of these lavishly embroidered clothes are intended for men. Women can wear sumptuous dresses only during their first year of marriage before the first baby arrives; after that, they are doomed to subdued colours and nearly total absence of ornament. Today, many of the country's women are wearing the veil again.

After a delicious lunch of shashlik and fresh fruit, we begin our long drive deep into the Kyzyl Kum desert outside Bukhara to visit a semi-nomadic Kazak family. In the semi-darkness of their cool *yurta*, a tent made from animal skins, I realize that Central Asia is more than the winding streets of Khiva and Bukhara and the numerous tourist haunts. Andrusha and I are sitting on a worn carpet in the company of three women of the Kakbaev family whose names sound exotic and hard to pronounce – Zyuragul, Zubiida and Umedgul. Their impassive sunburnt faces, measured movements and simple loose dresses speak of their quiet inner dignity. They barely know any Russian and can only guess why I and the others are here and what all this commotion is about. Yet they seem unfazed and composed. They treat us to *kumis*, camel's milk; it tastes awful, like sour cow's milk. Andrusha and I glance at each other but drink it anyway. We also drink tea and eat the freshly baked, flat scorched bread called *tanur*.

I want to know more about them – whether life is treating them well. They are quite satisfied, they tell me. In the present circumstances they are looked upon as well off with their two hundred sheep, fifty camels and countless hens and other poultry.

Every two weeks they slaughter three rams for meat. Milk is abundant, and they grow their own herbs. They are doing what they always did – producing and selling milk and meat. Theirs is a large family. I do not see the men – they are out working. Although Bukhara is only 30 miles away, the influence of the city is not felt here. I don't know whether that's good or bad. For many years the Soviet government brainwashed us into thinking that a positive aspect of socialism was the removal of barriers between town and countryside. Sitting on this carpet in a *yurta* one wonders how, despite years of pounding propaganda, this simple, ancient, free way of life has survived. One can only thank God that it has. Those who live in these vast, open spaces, on daily terms with the infinite, are blessed. Their environment imparts to them the conviction that everything under the sky is right and just.

As the filming draws to an end we make our way back to our van, which is surrounded by camels lazily grazing on the grass. The eldest of the sisters, Zyuragul, shares her grief with me – she is almost twenty-seven and still unmarried.

'Why?' I ask. 'Haven't you found the right person?'

'Well, probably I am not beautiful.' She shrugs her shoulders in embarrassment and perplexity. I encourage her, telling her she has a beautiful smile.

Their life may seem a simple one, but they breathe this hot, luxurious air perfumed with herbs and watch fabulous sunsets. I remember and savour the time when I lived deep in the country-side during the first five years of my life, while my beloved Leningrad was under siege. My mother took me into the depths of the forest where we lived in natural surroundings. I can understand these Kazak people; there is beauty in the simplicity of their lives.

After another overnight journey our train will arrive in the legendary Samarkand, situated in the Zevrashan valley. Sitting in my compartment, I read James Elroy Flecker's poetic tribute, written in 1922, called 'The Hungry Steppe':

Sweet to ride forth at evening from the wells,
When shadows pass gigantic on the sand,
And softly through the silence beat the bells
Along the Golden Road to Samarkand.

We travel not for trafficking alone;
By hotter winds our fiery hearts are fanned:
For lust of knowing what should not be known,
We take the Golden Road to Samarkand.

We awake in Samarkand. Venturing into the city is like stepping into a vividly-coloured dream, with exotic fruits, flowing silks and cerulean blue domes lending their hues to the swirling confusion of colour. Samarkand today is a unique blend of legend and history. In olden times the capital of several powerful states, it has been called the 'Eden of the Orient' and the 'Glittering summit of the world'; Tamerlane called it the 'eye and star of the earth'.

Ruy de Clavijo, a Spanish traveller who visited Tamerlane's court, wrote this in his journal: 'As I was approaching Samarkand, I searched to find a metaphor to describe its beauty. And I said, "Samarkand is like the colour of the sky, with its palaces shining like stars, and its streams flowing like the Milky Way!" and everybody liked what I said.'

The architectural monuments are breathtaking in their bold design; the graceful lines of slender, lancet arches perfectly counterpoint the semi-spherical domes, and every surface is made beautiful with decorated ceramic work, more dazzling in blue than the sober browns of Bukhara. Each ancient monument is a testimony to events, actual or imaginary. One such is the Guri-Emir ('Grave of the Emir') mausoleum, which is especially beautiful with its colourful mosaics, majestic fluted dome covered with blue tiles, and high vaults glittering with gold. Tamerlane, known locally as Timur, and his closest relatives lie buried here. In the centre are four gravestones fenced off on all sides. One of them is very strange – ominously black (the others are of white marble) and of a weird shape. When you look closer, you can see that it is made of dark green nephrite rather than black marble. This is Tamerlane's grave. Many wanted to possess this highly symbolic and precious stone. Nazir Shah even tried to take it away to Persia, but succeeded only in breaking off several pieces. The sarcophagus remained in place – a magnificent and sombre symbol of the vanity of life and eternity of beauty embodied in the precious stone and the perfect lines of the tomb.

The most impressive sight in Samarkand is the famous Registan Square (which means 'Place of Sand'), with its dazzling blue domes and huge madrassahs. On three sides the square is bordered by majestic structures: the Ulughbek madrassah (1417–20), the Sherdor madrassah (1619–36) and the Tillya-Kari madrassah (1647–60). The Ulughbek madrassah originally had fifty dormitory cells housing over a hundred students; the Sherdor ('Bearing Lions') is a mirror image of the Ulughbek. The Tillya-Kari closes Registan Square from the north; its name means 'Gilded' and, besides being an educational establishment, it also serves as a grand mosque. When we enter this exquisite mosque we find the interior is a blaze of gold. We are told that, when restoration work was being carried out, some of the workmen purposely started a fire so as to steal some of the gold used in the gilding, which they then claimed had been destroyed in the flames. Outside in the courtyard the aesthetic feast continues, and we buy wonderful hand-made ceramic plates and boxes.

My oriental impressions would be incomplete if we did not visit an open-air bazaar, so we go to a huge, riotous, cacophonously noisy market redolent with the aroma of spices. It is a striking contrast to the beggarly flea-market at the Gostinny Dvor in St Petersburg or the Arbat stalls in Moscow. There, the people seem desperate and nervous, money their only concern, while here they are friendly and happy to bargain. As I walk along the endless counters enjoying the lavish displays of wonderful fruit – sweet grapes, juicy peaches, fragrant melons and purple pomegranates – I feel as though I'm in a museum, feasting my eyes on a magnificent series of still lifes. Suddenly, I hear my name shouted amid the impossible din of the bazaar: 'Makarova! You are Natasha.' I raise my eyes to meet a glittering smile revealing two rows of gold dentures, kind and smiling eyes, and a huge hat in the timeless oriental fashion. This tomato seller remembers me from Leningrad – my fan, he had never missed a single ballet. We meet again, some twenty-three years later, in a bazaar in Samarkand. It smacks of a soap opera.

He has no flowers, so he hands me a huge tomato that I start to eat at his counter to please him. I do not ask him how it happens that he, who had trained as an engineer, is selling tomatoes here. He, in turn, doesn't ask me whether I am still on stage. We are glad to meet like two old friends with the past to share.

Next to this bazaar stands the Bibi Khanyam, the grand mosque, decorated with majolica mosaics, carved marble and gilt. The buildings of the main mosque and the two smaller ones were already beginning to crumble in Tamerlane's time. A devastating earthquake in the 1970s did further damage, and it has not yet been restored to its former beauty. The legend goes that Tamerlane's favourite Chinese wife planned the mosque as a gift to her husband on his return from one of his Indian campaigns; but the architect fell in love with her and refused to continue his work unless she agreed to accept his kiss. Eventually she did so and the mosque was completed. When Tamerlane returned, he saw the brand of passion on her cheek – he had the architect tortured and his wife hurled from the highest minaret. From then on, he ordered that all women should wear veils to shield men from the lure of their fatal attractions. With the resurgence of Muslim fundamentalism since the break-up of the Soviet Union, there is implicit irony in the fact that many women are now wearing the veil as an expression of national pride.

Tashkent

Passing through the Sanzar Pass or 'Tamerlane's Gate', between Samarkand and Tashkent, we see the railway builder's tribute which reads: 'In 1895 Tsar Nicholas II commanded that there be a railway. By 1898 it was done.' It was the railways which secured the colonial hold on Central Asia, an ambition asserted in the words of Dostoyevsky: '. . . with an aspiration for Asia, our spirit and forces will be regenerated'.

Sadly, Tashkent is the last point on this journey. In many respects it is an ordinary city, yet it holds a place of its own in the history of Russian culture. It is here that the great Russian actress Vera Komiusarzhevskaya died of smallpox in 1910; and it is here that the great poetess Anna Akhmatova lived during the Second World War. Yet, for the Russians, Tashkent was always considered a foreign land, an outpost of the great empire, the back yard that would become home, an unexpectedly discovered paradise. Many who settled here felt the strain of living among foreign people and a language they did not know – to survive, they had to sharpen their feeling of national identity.

As I arrive in Tashkent, I am excited to see my old classmate from the Vaganova ballet school in St Petersburg, Margarita Okatova, standing on the platform in the pouring rain with her fourteen-year-old ballerina daughter holding a beautiful bouquet of roses. I hop off the train and run to hug her, the two of us jumping up and down like children. It is an amazing turn of events for us to meet at this end of the world. I knew she had moved here, but I never expected to come to Tashkent myself. I remember her in school as a talented girl with an uncontrollable character. She would always surprise us, and particularly the school authorities, by her unrestrained behaviour. Our teacher, Shiripina, went so far as to say, 'Okatova, you need to have two policemen around you while you do your exercises.' Perhaps she was difficult to handle because she came from an orphanage. She is a few years older than I am, and while we were growing up she taught me a lot! Many years have passed since our schooldays, and I long to find the time just to sit with her, drink some vodka and let our thoughts drift back to the past. But I am only here for a day and the filming cannot wait. We have to stick to a very strict schedule.

Andrusha and I find ourselves in the home of Shukhrat and

Rasika Makhmudov and their two beautiful daughters, both around my son's age. They are a famous couple: Shukhrat directs documentaries and Rasika writes scenarios. They both studied in Moscow, at the Cinematography Institute. For twenty years they have been working at the Uzbek film studios where people look up to them as talented, uncompromising and serious masters. Hedrick Smith made them the heroes of his well-known book *The New Russians*, though they are not truly Russians – they are in fact Uzbeks.

Their films include *The Crimson Land*, about the disgraceful Afghanistan war, *The Boomerang*, about drug addicts, *The Flame*, about Uzbek women who immolated themselves, and *Islam*, about the spread of fundamentalism in Central Asia. I am especially interested in the latter two subjects. *The Flame* was prompted by an official order from the authorities for a film to be made to mark the anniversary of Khujun, the women's liberation movement in the East in the mid-twenties, when women discarded their black veils and burned them to show they were no longer anyone's property. This was described by the official press as one of the greatest achievements of Soviet power.

But the film Shukhrat made was not the film the authorities expected. Instead he exposed what was completely unknown to the outside world – the self-immolation of thousands of women during the eighties in protest against their unbearable lives, a practice which continues to this day. 'These women spent their lives primarily in the kitchen, where kerosene was always available to them,' Shukhrat explained. 'They would pour it over themselves and light a match. They would run out on the street like flaming torches screaming for help, but to save them was almost impossible – few survived.' Shukhrat interviewed some of them as they lay dying. Their testimonies were absolutely identical – poverty, early marriage and an unbearable subservient existence. The official death certificates describe the cause of death as 'clumsiness when dealing with fire'. It is tragic that their last desperate statement of protest is falsified. My God, what level of despair these women must reach to choose such an agonizing death. 'They were deprived of love,' Shukhrat said thoughtfully.

I ask about Shukhrat and Rasika's latest film, which deals with Islam in Uzbekistan and the way its extreme fundamentalist forms are affecting this nation. They explain that, since the fall of the socialist regime, the present-day government of Uzbekistan, mostly comprised of former Communist Party leaders, has been using Islam and the Uzbeks' nationalistic tendencies to manipulate the people. 'Islam in Uzbekistan is not simply promoted – it is imposed on us as an official ideology that crushes everything around us,' says Shukhrat. 'Rasika would not be able to work as a film editor if she were not working with me. Our daughters are picked on at school for wearing jeans, and we fear that there is no future for them in this country as modern, free-thinking young women. New mosques and Islamic schools have been opened, and the Koran has become the main curriculum in all the educational establishments. Of course, the Uzbek fundamentalists are a far cry from the Iranian fanatics, yet the trend is there to see. This has become a threat hanging over the Russian as well as the Uzbek intelligentsia.' As honest documentary filmmakers, they risk losing their jobs. Not one of their latest films has appeared on TV, while *Islam* has been banned outright.

In the evening I go to the Ilkhom Theatre (Uzbek for 'inspiration'), which is one of the city's cultural centres. Founded in 1976 outside the government-subsidized state system, which at that time was an almost impossible thing to do, it survived despite an avalanche of blows from above. The company staged Bertolt Brecht, Evgeni Schwartz and Alexander Vampilov, as well as contemporary playwrights who were banned from the official academic theatres. This underground theatre became the centre of cultural opposition, where the truth was told even though it was concealed in veiled metaphors. Now much has changed in life and the theatre – there is no longer a threat of mental hospitals and prisons for those who speak the truth.

One of the company's latest productions is called *The Class Concert*. It is an eclectic piece in which young actors perform ballet exercises, mime, fencing and dance intermingled with text. The youngest performer is a ballerina of thirteen, the age at which I too started ballet. She catches my gaze. What a joy to see such spirituality emanating from her enlightened face. Suddenly, to my surprise, she comes to me, curtsies and takes my hand, leading me to the stage. I suddenly feel the desire to move, to improvise, and she follows me. This kind of duet brings me back to my earliest days of ballet; it seems like yesterday. I wonder what lies ahead for her – I hope I will hear of her in ten years' time. Will she have a creative life and bring joy to people and enlighten them through her art? She has all the potential to do so. After the performance, I discover that her name is Natalia (Natasha) too.

Tashkent slides past the windows, scarcely discernible behind a remorseless downpour of rain. Beaten both by weather and our harassing schedule, we decide to forgo sightseeing and make silent promises to ourselves to save this pleasure for another time. Another time? I wonder if that will ever be. This moment carries its own finality; it can never be repeated. But I have always been a fatalist, and know that I shall be in Tashkent again if my destiny so ordains.

From beginning to end this whole journey has been imbued with a dream-like quality, the familiar and the strange jostling for space, my consciousness besieged by buried memories one moment, new discoveries the next. I ought to feel at home in Russia, the country of my childhood, the land to which my pulse responds, and indeed I sometimes do. It has been magical and moving to hear again my native Russian tongue spoken all around me, enveloping me in its musical embrace – such a lovely, expressive language. The experience has reminded me how much I owe to my motherland, to the values I learned to cherish in my upbringing and to the training which fashioned me and gave me such wonderful opportunities.

This journey has satisfied a deep and crucial need. It has been a kind of personal pilgrimage, a homage to my roots and nurturing. And yet, at the same time, I have to recognize that I have occasionally felt an alien in my own land, and not simply because I have changed so much since I left it. The feeling of detachment runs profoundly in my soul and in my artistry. As an artist, I have never felt constrained, defined or excluded by geographical boundaries. Art is universal; it speaks no single language, nor does it acknowledge any single nationality. It is beyond and above politics. My life as a ballerina crossed all frontiers, and my dance floor was the world itself.

As I said at the outset, before this journey began, I have been fortunate to have lived in both East and West, to have straddled separate cultures and been nourished by different influences. I am intensely proud to be Russian, and at the same time I feel international, free from the ligature of limited identity and able to soar above the artificial restraints of nationality. It has been a touching and moving experience for me to watch my son Andrusha begin to soar, too, as the adventure of travelling into unknown territory has freed his spirit and kindled his inspiration. He is no longer *only* an American, but something more besides. We have visited places together, many of them as new to me as they were to him, especially in Central Asia, and joined one another in discovery. He is my son not only by blood, but in spirit, too, as he now shows the same need to explore and expand, to look and learn, above all to deny the smothering restrictions of prescribed dogma.

As I said earlier, I am a fatalist. I believe we were meant to be here, that nothing happens by chance, and that this shared experience with my son was not a random event brought about by a mere telephone call. Of course I have made decisions in life, many of them momentous, but I have always reached them intuitively rather than by intellectual reasoning, and they have generally been right. I have been guided by providence, a beneficent fate which also decreed that we should go to Russia and to Asia, that we should encounter some people, miss others, be touched by the ripples of my past, and record it all on film. However the film turns out, it was not an accident that we made it, not a simple professional decision in response to an invitation. It was meant to be. It is part of the all-embracing whole of destiny, of the mysterious yet invigorating and ennobling pattern of self-discovery and self-renewal.

DERRY TO KERRY
A VOYAGE OF DISCOVERY

Michael Palin

Michael Palin's journey from Derry to Kerry

Ireland is a great place. A great place for myths and confusions and misunderstandings. Facts and figures are, of course, quite acceptable, but should not be allowed to intrude on real life. So let's get them out of the way early.

The island known as Ireland covers an area of 32,588 square miles. It has been, since 1921, divided into two countries. Northern Ireland, known as Ulster or the Province, comprises the six counties of the north-east, and is part of the United Kingdom. Its capital is Belfast. The other twenty-six counties form the Republic of Ireland, also known as Eire, whose capital is Dublin. The total population of Ireland is just over 5 million. Roughly 1.5 million live in Northern Ireland and 3.5 million in the Republic. Seventy million Irish live abroad. Those are the facts, now for what really happened . . .

Even the Irish are not sure if they have any railways. When the subject comes up in conversation (which is almost an Irish national sport) it is met with polite puzzlement, as if you'd asked for the population of Kurdistan or the last time West Ham won the FA Cup. To be helpful, and the Irish love to be helpful, they may recollect hearing of a line between Belfast and Dublin, but rarely will they know of anyone who's ever travelled on it. It's clear that any railway journey around Ireland will be something of a challenge, requiring keen detective work.

Whilst learning about the railways I hope also to learn a little more about my Irish great-grandmother, Brita Gallagher. Family legend has it that she was orphaned in the Potato Famines of the 1840s. The facts are that she was born in 1844, that she ended up in America, and that she was seventeen years and six months old when she stole the heart of Edward Palin, a thirty-five-year-old Oxford college don on a walking holiday in the Swiss Alps.

A straight line from Derry to Kerry would run for some 250 miles. It would also effectively divide railway and non-railway Ireland. Though at one time there were two hundred separate railway companies in Ireland, and a network which once covered three and a half thousand miles, there is now hardly a piece of track left to the west of the Derry–Kerry divide. Any railway journey between the two places has to go via the capital cities of Belfast and Dublin, which is fine if you want to see Ireland but pretty hopeless if your granny's ill.

Derry itself, the second city of Northern Ireland, could, in 1930, boast four termini serving four different railway companies – the Midland, the Great Northern and, from the west, the Londonderry and Lough Swilly and the Donegal Railway. Today it is reduced to just one featureless, modern station and a seven-times-daily service to the outside world.

But history is not something easily forgotten on this island and the spirit of the Donegal Railway lives on beside the broad, swift waters of the River Foyle, where two miles of track have been laid over the last four years by the North-West of Ireland Railway Society, the start of an ambitious scheme to reopen a railway link with the wild, remote and beautiful county of Donegal. I travelled on it aboard a short, chunky diesel railcar, vintage 1934, filled with nuns and schoolchildren, which deposited me at the brand-new Foyle Road Station and Transport Museum, funded by a £300,000 grant from the EC. It's ironic that the Brussels bureaucrats should be so generous to a railway service that doesn't exist any more.

On the hill above Foyle Road Station rise the grey-walled ramparts of the city, started in 1613 when Derry was colonized by the Irish Society, a group of London merchant companies, and first became known as Londonderry. The walls are solid, well preserved and still in use. The old fortifications are now themselves fortified with the steel mesh, armour plating, razor wire and concrete of today's watchtowers, rising a blank and bulbous like giant mushrooms newly sprouted on the skyline. The most recent wave of Troubles began here with the civil rights marches of Bernadette Devlin and others in the late 1960s and spiralled almost out of control after thirteen civilians were shot dead by paratroops in the Bogside area on what became known as 'Bloody Sunday' – 30 January 1972. It comes as a shock to remember that this city, so constantly and expensively observed by Army and police, combed regularly by foot patrols and heavily armoured vehicles, is as much a part of the United Kingdom as York or Southsea. Perhaps it's even more of a shock to learn that, in a poll commissioned by the BBC in 1988, its inhabitants voted Londonderry amongst the dozen 'best planned and greenest cities' in the country. The mood here is optimistic. The city council will talk less about the three thousand deaths in Northern Ireland since the Troubles began and more about the four thousand new houses built in Derry in four years. Rather than talk of sectarian confrontation, they will point to the democratic power-sharing agreements which mean that this year's Mayor of Derry, a 70 per cent Catholic city, happens to be a member of Ian Paisley's hardline Protestant Democratic Unionist Party. They will tell you of the European and American money being invested here.

Considering that fifteen years ago a quarter of the buildings in Derry had suffered some damage from civil violence, the regeneration is remarkable and admirable. But ask the reasons for this improvement and the answer will not be reconciliation. The two sides have agreed to live apart. The Protestants who call their city Londonderry have moved away to the east bank of the Foyle, leaving the Catholics who call their city Derry more entrenched and less threatened on the west. The schizoid nature of the city remains in the firm retention of its two names, both of which are loaded with significance. There have been attempts to have it both ways – Londonderry-stroke-Derry – which merely led to it being risibly referred to as 'Stroke City'.

Northern Ireland Railways does not equivocate – the name on the station sign is Londonderry. The rolling stock is unexciting – blue-and-yellow-liveried three-coach diesel sets, exactly the same as all the others that cover Northern Ireland. Occasionally, if there is a demand, they will join two together, but basically, apart from the express service from Belfast to Dublin, that's it. Fortunately, the good old days of Ulster railways, when four thousand people were employed instead of barely eight hundred now, can still be experienced two or three times a summer, courtesy of the Railway Preservation Society of Ireland, and I'm lucky to catch the first Steam Special of the year, running out of Londonderry to Coleraine and Belfast.

Ex-railwaymen have turned out for a nostalgic wallow. I get talking to a barrel of a man who used to be a fireman in the steam days. Railways unite countries, he reckons. They bring people together. The love of railways is non-sectarian. The genuine train enthusiast is above that sort of thing. Which is not to say he can avoid it. My friend turns away from the bland modern station and points across the street to an imposing stone building with a tall, Italianate tower. It used to be Londonderry Station until a terrorist bomb blew it apart in 1975. Northern Ireland Railways didn't consider it worth rebuilding. Fortunately, someone else did.

The ten-coach excursion is packed, the atmosphere that of a school treat. The locomotive, resplendent in eye-catching pale-blue livery, is, as it should be, the centre of attention. It's a modestly sized, elegant 4–4–0 which looks as if its name should be James or Edward, but is, in fact, *Slieve Gullion*, after a mountain in Armagh. It was built eighty years ago for Great Northern Railways, in the days when Ireland was still one country. With a piercing blast on the whistle and with great thumping breaths of grey smoke it pulls its considerable and appreciative audience out along the River Foyle heading in the only direction the railways go from Derry these days – east. Another ex-railwayman, Tom McDevitte, has some good stories of the old steam days. Though he wasn't meant for the footplate he once stood in for a fireman with such conspicuous lack of success that, at one point, the train was overtaken by a butterfly. He has distinct memories, too, of a level crossing where a goat used to stand in the middle of the track, impervious to any bells, shouts and blasts on the whistle. The only way it could be induced to move was by throwing large lumps of coal in its direction. When enough coal had been thrown an old lady would emerge, collect up the coal and call the goat in.

As 'Stroke City' slips away to the south-west we're into wide, low-lying flatland beside Lough Foyle, and horses, sheep and cows, used to the comfortable rumble of diesels, are scattering at our approach. It's the sort of scene which used to be reproduced as graphic evidence of the evil of railways by nineteenth-century farmers who blamed trains for everything from terminating pregnancies to tainting the milk. The gorse is fresh and thick along the side of the track, a golden ribbon following our progress. *Slieve Gullion* gathers speed and healthy respect as we rattle and swing under bridges and over crossings, at every one a cluster of admirers. If you waved at cars you'd be put away, but waving at railway trains is seen as evidence of sanity and decency.

I leave the Steam Special at Portrush – the popular coastal resort they call Northern Ireland's Blackpool. The station has little *joie de vivre* about it. Rubbish-strewn and desolate, it could be a contender for a Worst-Kept Station Award. As I wander into the town I'm struck by the number of hairdressers in Portrush. They have names like Sophisticuts and Shylocks. At least they're open, which is more than can be said for the funfair or the substantial Station Hotel, in the neo-Tudor style, which appears to be totally abandoned, unless the breeze-blocked windows are some cut-price security device. In fact the only evidence of railway life in Portrush is Traks Nite Club at the end of the platform. Still, if you're prepared to hop on a bus, there's much to see along the north coast. There's sixteenth-century Dunluce Castle, perched so precipitously on the edge of a cliff that the kitchen once slipped into the sea as a meal was being prepared.

There's Bushmill's Whiskey Distillery and the Giant's Causeway, which Dr Johnson cryptically advised was 'worth seeing, but not worth going to see'. Then there's the shock of finding yourself, at Fair Head near Ballycastle, within swimming distance of Scotland, only twelve miles away. The swim is not recommended. Along these fine, languid headlands and wide bays are dotted a string of hotels and guest houses whose preference for breakfast delicacies like the Ulster Fry have earned this stretch the name of the Cholesterol Coast.

But if it's railways you're looking for, I can recommend a swift return to Coleraine and a fifty-five-minute ride down the Belfast line, alighting at the neat pillar-box red station at Antrim, where they still open and shut the level-crossing gates by hand, and making your way to Shanes Castle on the shores of Lough Neagh. Here you will find, if you're lucky, *Shane*, *Tyrone* or even *Nancy*. They are all locomotives run and cared for by Lord O'Neill, heir to one of the greatest names in Irish history, but, like the humblest train-spotter, deeply in love with railways. *Un*like the humblest train-spotter, Lord O'Neill can, if he spots a train he likes, bring it home and run it on the one and a half miles of track laid through the picturesque woodlands of his estate. What has particularly caught his eye over the years are locos and rolling stock from the small but significant 3-foot (91-cm) gauge railways which could once be found all over Ireland. *Shane* used to pull trainloads of peat, or turf as the Irish call it, across the bogs to Portarlington Power Station. Now it pulls Toytown coaches carrying the tourists on whom much of Lord O'Neill's expensive hobby depends. His Shanes Castle Railway has two coats of arms now – one a crown, a fish and the Red Hand of Ulster, the other a castle, bird in flight and locomotive rampant. Lord O'Neill, a most unstuffy peer, is a touch embarrassed by this opportunist piece of heraldry: 'The marketing people said we ought to . . . you know how it is.'

From Antrim the main line runs beside the broad, empty M2 motorway, with which it can hardly hope to compete, and terminates at Central Station, Belfast – a squat modern fortress set on the outside of the city centre. If you've read the history of Ulster railways and seen what the old Great Northern terminus at Great Victoria Street used to look like, and the Belfast and Northern Counties terminus at York Road, and the Belfast and County Down's at Queen's Quay – all elegantly decorated neoclassical buildings – you can only grieve at the loss.

This is rather how it is with Belfast. The bombs of the seventies and early eighties have left some scars, and the redevelopment which followed has left some more, but the shadow of Victorian prosperity still hangs over the city, from the massive hulks of the old linen mills on the Shankill Road to the towering copper dome of the marble-filled City Hall.

As in Derry, the casual visitor is struck by the evidence of military occupation – the foot patrols, the grey armour-plated police vehicles, the soldiers raking the streets through telescopic sights – but perhaps even more struck by the way life in Belfast goes on around it. The locals are patient, friendly and unapologetic. They're proud of their city and full of information. As we head to my hotel the taxi driver observes, 'D'you know, you must be the first person I've taken today from Central Station to Central Station. Did you know that?' I suspect it's the prelude to a joke, but in fact it's a bit of local history – the old Central Station stood on land now occupied by my destination, the Europa Hotel. Shaped like a slightly bent iron bar, this relic of the sixties has the uncoveted title of being the most bombed hotel in Europe. I've stayed here on many occasions and have suffered nothing worse than an Ulster welcome and ensuing hangover, but its unenviable record continues. Just three weeks after my stay a 1000 lb (454 kg) IRA bomb blew out most of the windows. I'm told that if you're there when it's hit they give you a special tie.

I like the Europa because it is stubbornly resistant to intimidation and up-market glossiness. It is the centre for much of the social life of this resilient city – which has become a progressively more lively place in the thirteen years I've known it. I first came here to appear in the annual Festival, whose reputation is known and envied far and wide. I'd been lured by the chance of performing my first one-man show. From what I knew of such things the key to the show was speed – quick changes, no hanging about. I rehearsed for weeks and brought the show to such a peak of perfection that on opening night at the Arts Theatre my one-and-a-half-hour show ran exactly thirty-five minutes. There was nothing to do but take the audience into my confidence. I apologized, suggested they all drank as much as they could in the interval, and that we did the second half together. In the end I was saved by their generosity and quickness of wit. I've been a great admirer of Belfast audiences ever since.

There *is* a railway connection to all this. Apart from the fact that the Arts Theatre is built above a station and there's always a laugh to be gained when the 21.38 to Lisburn trundles through in the middle of a joke, I would never have come here if Michael Barnes, the Festival Administrator, had not been a railway fan. Michael usually lures me to some railway venue whenever I'm in town, and this time we are allowed a sneak preview of the new transport collection at the Ulster Folk and Transport Museum, gathered beneath an uncompromisingly modern single-span shed, 300 feet (91 metres) long and 100 feet (31 metres) high, which lies like a giant maggot in the soft wooded hills above Belfast Lough.

The only locomotive undaunted by this huge shed is No. 800, a magnificent three-cylinder 4–6–0, dating back to 1939 and lone survivor of the three largest railway engines ever built in Ireland. It's called *Maeve*, after some avenging Irish heroine in the Boadicea mould. Aside from *Maeve* the engines look quite old-fashioned, with stove-pipe chimneys and outside bells, generally much smaller than you would find in a British transport collection. I'm reminded once again that, though the Irish railways were once so diverse, their longest routes ran less than two hundred miles across largely flat agricultural country one-tenth as full of people as Britain. There was no need for giants.

I think it was at the museum that I first heard the name of William Dargan. I had recommended to one of the directors a book I was reading – R. F. Foster's *Modern Ireland* – but he returned it to me rather severely after a cursory glance at the index. 'Six hundred pages and not a mention of Dargan ... typical!' At the time I thought this an outburst of professional jealousy, but the more I got to know about Dargan the more convinced I became that history had not dealt justly with a man who was the Brunel *and* Stephenson of Irish railways. Thanks to him there was a railway line out of Dublin before there was one out of London. The Dublin to Kingstown railway was only the third regular passenger line in the world (Stockton–Darlington and Liverpool–Manchester being the first and second). Dargan went on from there to design, construct and very often fund nearly a thousand miles of track. He was talented, energetic and enormously productive, but some bad career moves in later life – he lost heavily in financing the Dublin Exhibition of 1851 and turned down Queen Victoria's personal offer of a knighthood – might have blotted his copybook. He died, after a fall from his horse, in 1867.

Feeling myself sinking too unhealthily into the past, I combine a day trip to the seaside with a look at the railways of the present, taking one of the frequent trains that run from Belfast Central to Bangor. The standard three-coach diesel rumbles out over the River Lagan, under a motorway, and then swings past the Harland and Wolff shipyards where the *Titanic* was built. The massive cranes, Goliath and Samson, dominate the city skyline – a reminder, as they trundle majestically back and forth, that heavy industry in Britain is not quite dead.

We pass close by Belfast's City Airport, which is part of the Short's aerospace complex. Once again the name triggers more reminders of the past than of the present. The Sunderland flying boat was made here. Like Harland and Wolff, Short's have received large amounts of government money to stay in business. Politically – and almost any initiative in Northern Ireland is scoured for its political significance – these subsidies are seen to favour the traditionally Protestant-dominated industries of East Belfast. It is remarkable only to an outsider that the most recent

Labour Force Survey indicates that 24 per cent of Roman Catholic men and 10 per cent of Protestant men are out of work.

At Helen's Bay I'm in stockbroker country, five miles from Belfast, where wealth brings space and space brings tolerance. Here, set back in leafy lanes, is a world away from the Falls and Shankill Roads. Doubtless there is pain and anger here too, behind the picture windows at the end of the long driveways, but it's personal and private, not public and political. The profusion of big, comfortable houses on this well-wooded hillside does not indicate a country unable to cope. Life goes on, and, judging by the sleek German cars on the winding roads and the brilliant white yachts in the harbour at Bangor, it's a pretty good life for some. Obviously the opportunist who built the railway line out on to this picturesque peninsula had spotted that too. Back in Belfast I find out his name from the helpful people at Central Station. It's William Dargan.

One of the most precious cargoes on Irish railways is the Guinness that comes up to Belfast from the brewery in Dublin. 'Belfast drinks a trainload of Guinness a day,' they tell me, and I can think of no better way to subsidize the railways than putting a rich, smooth glassload away, surrounded by the tiles and sparkling stained glass of the Crown Bar – a Victorian gin palace in the centre of Belfast and the only pub owned by the National Trust.

I must be drunk because I'm beginning to philosophize. This is greatly encouraged in Ireland. There is no stigma attached to a wandering train of thought provided it amuses the company. The enjoyment of Ireland, I suggest, with the finality of one who has been here almost a week, is rather akin to the enjoyment of a Guinness. It cannot be hurried. It requires an investment of time and patience. Everyone, addict and first-timer alike, must respect the minute or two it takes for a Guinness to settle – for the grainy brown to coalesce into deep black and the muddy froth to focus into richest cream. Even then it's not for knocking back, it's for ruminating with. Like Ireland, the benefits are reflective not aggressive. That there are, in this country, those who would lob bombs into places where Guinness is being drunk, and then justify it as historically inevitable, is still something I cannot begin to understand.

To try to learn more I visit the tribal areas of the Falls and Shankill with a man prominent in Belfast commerce, Ivor Oswald. Like anywhere else immortalized only in stories of violence one half-expects to see horns sticking out of people's heads as our car crosses the motorway, goes past the Divis Flats, and into the Falls Road. What in fact you see are joggers and fathers pushing prams and children in uniform coming out of school and old ladies shopping. The only people diving for cover are the Army patrols deploying their way into the massively fortified Andersonstown Road Police Station. What is abnormal about the Falls Road is the excellence of some of its facilities. The Royal Hospital, because of its location, has developed some on the most advanced trauma surgery techniques in the world; St Louise's Comprehensive is the biggest single-sex school in Europe, and is responsible for some of the best academic results in the city; and there are award-winning housing schemes based not on concrete but on respect for the traditional red brick of Belfast.

Alongside all this there is plenty of evidence of violently held beliefs. Many buildings are protected by steel-mesh fencing, and some targets, like the dole office, by more than that. The public buses have been such a target for hijackings and burnings that many people travel in London-style black cabs which cruise up and down the Falls Road, picking up people as they go for a flat fee of a few shillings. Streets have been unofficially retitled with names of Gaelic or even paramilitary significance, of which my favourite, in a creepy kind of way, is RPG Avenue (Rocket Propelled Grenade Avenue). There is an uncomfortable beauty, too, to the painted walls: a Madonna and Child; a peeling likeness of Bobby Sands, who died on a hunger strike in 1981; a romantic depiction of the IRA members shot and killed by British soldiers in Gibraltar; and of course the slogans: 'Peace With Justice', 'Our Day Will Come'.

The only place I know which resembles, in any way, the 100 per cent Catholic Nationalist community around the Falls is the 100 per cent Protestant, Loyalist community of the Shankill Road. Perhaps they hate each other because their conditions are so similar. Shankill too has its black cabs, its proliferation of churches, its clutch of new shopping malls, and its own slogans: 'No Surrender' and 'This We Shall Maintain'. It too has elaborately-painted walls. Only the emblems are different. Here it's the Union Jack rather than the Virgin Mary, the Red Hand of Ulster rather than the tricolour of the Republic.

Ivor Oswald refuses to be downcast by what he sees, even as we sit inside our car looking out in drizzling rain at the Peace Line, a relentlessly ugly, grimly fortified wall which runs between the two communities like a badly-stitched wound.

'Each side has its own culture, its own tradition, and no one should deny the fact that these communities have a vibrancy and a life of their own. But in reality you're looking at two traditions, two cultures, two nationalities and that is the essence of the problem. It's a national identity crisis that we all suffer from.'

'And they shall never be one?'

'They will not be one in my lifetime.' He pauses, uncomfortable to be sitting under the nose of the security forces. 'But within each community one has to recognize there's a lot of work going on, a lot of regeneration going on, and cross-community relations are developing on each side to respect the traditions and culture of the other.'

Next day, as the three o'clock diesel-drawn 'Enterprise' service pulls out of Central Station for Dublin, I can see away to my left concrete evidence of Belfast's regeneration in the half-finished supports of the biggest rail project in Ulster since the Second World War – the Cross-Harbour Rail Link. One and a half miles of new track, including a three-quarter mile bridge over the river, is due to open in November 1994. For the first time the two halves of Northern Ireland's railway system will be united, and a new Great Victoria Street Station will open a year later.

In addition, £80 million-worth of investment is to be spent

on upgrading the 113 miles of line between Belfast and Dublin. It will be no TGV but, with speeds of 90 miles an hour possible, the current 2 hour 15 minute journey time will be reduced to an hour and a half. Most significantly, the trains currently operated half by Northern Ireland Railways and half by Irish Rail (Iarnród Éireann) will share a livery – an outward and visible sign of the railway as a symbol of cross-border cooperation. It won't be the first time the railway has been used as such a symbol. At the end of the 1980s the line was frequently disrupted by terrorist activity. More often than not no damage was done, but it became very common for the train to be stopped and the line searched whilst long-suffering passengers were bused into the Republic. Confidence and passenger levels fell. It was at this point that a number of individuals in the North and South decided that they were not going to stand idly by and watch the life-blood squeezed out of this precious link. Two of them travel down with me today, across the green pastureland and through grey, unsmiling towns like Lurgan and Portadown. Sam McAughtry is a writer from Belfast, a keen, wry, articulate man with a mane of silver hair grown to an artist's length, and Chris Hudson is a Protestant trade union leader from Dublin – solid, amiable and persuasive. They fought the bombers with the power of the people, mobilizing large numbers of city-dwellers in the two capital cities to take the train across the border and dare the terrorists to stop them. They called it the Peace Train – and its success was such that they still run it four years on.

We enter the close-packed hills of South Armagh. This is Rupert Bear country, with gentle slopes, quilted with dry-stone walls, scattered with blossom from the may and hawthorn trees waving in the wind. It's also bandit country and the scars show. There are houses and gardens with swings, and there are houses burnt out and walls scrawled with slogans. My last image of Northern Ireland is a church on a hill with a bride and groom and a long white wedding car waiting, whilst on the opposite hill an Army foot patrol, heads swivelling nervously, works its way past a sign advertising 'The Newry Golf Inn – Lunches and Teas'.

I spend most of the rest of the journey, beyond Dundalk and towards Drogheda, laughing. The Irish tell much better jokes about themselves than the English ever do, and never signal the punch-line, so I'm frequently caught out. The talk turns to drums and drumming, a very Irish phenomenon. There is still a tradition of marching with drums. 'There are,' Sam reckons, 'more bands per square mile in Northern Ireland than any other country.' But it's not what it was in the fifties. 'Och . . . you get the mushroom bands . . .,' he goes on.

'Mushroom bands?'

Chris translates, 'They come up overnight. Before the marching season begins on 12 July.'

There follows comparison of the Lambeg Drum, the biggest of them all, and the pride of the Orangemen, with the traditional Irish drum – the Bodhran.

'Best played with an open penknife,' someone remarks drily.

Things will be very different now we're in Southern Ireland, I'm told. I look outside expectantly. The station signs are in Gaelic and English, the police are called the Garda, the distances are in kilometres and the red letter-boxes have turned green. What is so different?

Sam explains patiently, 'As soon as Ireland entered the Common Market in 1972, they decided that from a certain date – 1 July maybe – all cars would switch to driving on the right-hand side of the road. If it was successful, buses and lorries would follow a year later.'

Both Chris and Sam, Dublin and Belfast, loved this one. I wrote it down, solemnly, like a news reporter.

At Drogheda we rumble across a girder bridge 95 feet (29 metres) above the River Boyne, and across dark shadows of Irish history. In 1649 Oliver Cromwell stormed and massacred the city of Drogheda with a degree of barbarity that has never been forgotten. Meanwhile the Protestant Loyalists, the most fanatical supporters of the union with Britain, celebrate an event which took place forty-one years later only three miles away – the Battle of the Boyne, when William of Orange, a Dutchman, defeated King James II and ensured the Protestant succession in England.

The Irish Sea can be glimpsed as a dull sheen of grey below drifting mist as we bustle through stations painted cream and blue with singular names like Balbriggan, Skerries and Rush and Lusk. Glimpse a beautiful old ironwork canopy at Malahide Station and then on under stout stone bridges and into gorse-filled cuttings. At Howth Junction we enter the first stretch of electrified railway on my journey so far. It's part of the DART (Dublin Area Rapid Transport) system which runs round Dublin bay, linking the city centre with Howth in the north and Bray in the south. From now on the stations, and most of the trains, we pass are painted in the distinctive moss-green DART livery. Maybe it's that distant drop of Irish blood, but I'm already feeling at home here.

Writers have a special cachet in the Republic. They're not only appreciated – they're encouraged. Highly advantageous tax incentives kept writers like Frederick Forsyth here, and of course Dublin has been home to a disproportionate number of the great practitioners – Jonathan Swift, Oscar Wilde, Sean O'Casey, George Bernard Shaw, Brendan Behan, Richard Brinsley Sheridan, James Joyce, Samuel Beckett and many more. In 1850 Anthony Trollope, then working for the Post Office, wrote most of *Barchester Towers* on the train between Dublin and Belfast.

Dublin is a good city to step out into, big enough to feel a little grand in and small enough to be able to see open country-side from the centre of town. Straight ahead of me are the walls of green-tinted glass which make up the brand-new Financial Centre – the latest glossy manifestation of corporate Ireland, enjoying its new-found independence within Europe. Beyond that the perfect proportions of James Gandon's classical Custom House reflect the eighteenth century, the hey-day of Ireland's dependence on England.

The River Liffey doesn't seem wide enough to split the city, yet there is still kudos to be had from living in the southern half.

Here are most of the fine buildings – the imposing and harmonious classical revival architecture of Trinity College, the elegant but unboastful seat of government at Leinster House, and the famous red-brick terraces of St Stephen's Green and Merrion Square. There are some fine buildings north of the Liffey, but you've only to compare the run-down state of Mountjoy Square – now a 'Tax Incentive Area' – with its Georgian counterparts to the south to notice the difference.

Dublin encourages the walker. The central area is compact, there are pubs every few yards, a minimum of irritating regulations (making rules is an English, not an Irish preoccupation) and the shops offer high browsing potential. No one will rush you, and the soft voice and smiles come naturally. You can slip very easily in and out of history. I visit Greene's bookshop, itself well over a hundred years old, which I find opposite the site of Finn's Hotel in which Nora Barnacle, James Joyce's beloved, used to work. I'm on the Dargan trail, but, after much searching, the proprietor of Greene's is very upset that he can find nothing on him at all. I tell him not to worry – Dargan is the Invisible Man of Irish history. I then walk round the corner and there, slap bang in front of the National Gallery of Ireland, astride a plinth, in modest, unstrutty pose, is none other than William Dargan. Apparently his statue was erected by public subscription in his lifetime – an unusual honour which suggests he was something of a people's hero. By the time I return to my hotel a package of faxed pages on Dargan is waiting for me – courtesy of Greene's bookshop.

Having now made a little progress in my quest for Dargan – born Carlow 1799; trained under the great Thomas Telford; kept his workers on during the Famine Years even when nothing left for them to do – it's time to prosecute the quest for Gallagher, my Irish great-granny. I have already been in contact with Tom Lindert, a professional genealogist, and we arrange to meet at the National Library, a fine but modest Victorian civic building tucked away behind the much grander Government Buildings, recently restored at the behest of Prime Minister

Charles Haughey for 18 million punts (about £18 million). When finished, Dubliners christened it the Chas Mahal. When Albert Reynolds became Prime Minister they changed it to the Albert Hall. The puncturing of pomposity is one of the most endearing qualities of the Dubliner. A very rich businessman decided to endow the city with a fine and expensive sculpture to be located on O'Connell Street. Designed to perpetuate the memory of his father, it took the form of a woman – Anna Livia, the spirit of the Liffey – complete with water tumbling artistically around her. No sooner was it put up than she became affectionately known as the Floozy in the Jacuzzi.

Tom has some news for me on the Gallagher front. His team, who have been employed by such great Irishmen as Ronald Reagan and John McEnroe, have come up with a copy of the certificate of marriage between Edward Palin and Brita Gallagher, which took place at the British Embassy in Paris in October 1867. There is no mention of Brita's parents, which Tom thinks unusual and probably points to an admission that she was indeed a famine orphan. Only four other people were present at the marriage, one of whom was the American woman, Caroline Watson, who adopted Brita. He spreads out a number of the parish records for the period 1844 to 1850. There are Gallaghers but no mention of a Brita. But did I know that Watson was an Irish name? I didn't until then. Tom has discovered one area of North Cork where Watsons and Gallaghers lived closely together. Maybe Caroline was family. There is only one way to find out.

My route to Gallagher country is going to have to take the long way round, for I have been offered an unmissable ride on the footplate' of a steam excursion along the south-east coast from Dublin to Rosslare. Overalls and a hat are supplied, and I report for duty at Connolly Station at 9.30 on a warm Sunday morning.

There are to be five of us on the footplate, and even with one getting off at Greystones – about twenty miles down the line – it'll be a squeeze. Apart from the driver, easily the oldest of us all, there is an assistant driver and a young trainee who's given up his Sunday as part of a steam-engine driver's course. I admire his dedication.

'You must love this.'

'No, I hate it. I have my twelve-year-old son playing in his school football final and I'm here because there's no one else.'

I promise to help him out, which seems to amuse everybody.

Once on the footplate I'm with a self-contained, laconic, hard-working little team whose sole aim is to get this fire-breathing beast to the end of the line. Their world has nothing to do with that of the passengers, who could have fallen out of the train and be hanging upside-down from the telegraph wires for all they care. The crew's entire concentration is on steam pressure levels and oil pressure levels and coal stock levels and lubricating pistons and sliding home dampers and keeping the fires blazing.

A locomotive like this takes some looking after. No. 461, a solid, unflashy black 2–6–0 goods engine, is no spring chicken. It was up and running seventy-two years ago. The fact that it is alive at all is thanks to the persistence of the Railway Preservation Society of Ireland, who rebuilt it from scratch in the 1980s.

Once we've been given the green flag, it's down to business. Off with the brake, ease the regulator, harness the steam, and whoever's not doing anything make the tea. Our departure from Connolly, humphing over Custom House Quay and across a hazy River Liffey with a dozen other bridges stretching away to the west, is just magnificent. On a day like today you couldn't wish to be anywhere else. Unless you're the trainee driver, of course, stoking coal and cursing his luck. Progress through Dublin is spectacular. The line never dives into cuttings or through tunnels, it rides through the city at rooftop level, like the 'El' in New York. There's an extra satisfaction to this first stretch of the route for we are riding on the oldest commuter railway in the world – Dublin to Kingstown, now called Dun Laoghaire (pronounced Dunleary). Passengers have been doing what we're doing ever since 17 December 1834, when a locomotive called *Hibernia* hauled the first of five thousand passengers who made the run on opening day.

Our route passes directly by Lansdowne Road Stadium where, three days before, the once highly unfancied Irish soccer team held the highly fancied Danes to a 1–1 draw. (Their opponents had been greeted with a huge banner: 'Welcome Denmark. We Wish You All the Best of Irish Luck'.) On past trim suburban bungalows, through Sydney Parade, and suddenly the chilly waters of the Irish Sea fill the horizon. Near here the line, William Dargan's first, nearly foundered after stubborn opposition from two big landowners – Lord Cloncurry and the Rev. Sir Harcourt Lees, who owned the land down to the sea at Blackrock. As the official history explains, however, 'with a promise to build a tunnel, a pair of towers with pathway leading to the strand, piers, bridges, a bathing pavilion, a mini-harbour and £3000 and £7500 by way of sweetener, they agreed to permit the intrusion'. I bet they did.

We seem to be flying along now, past Dun Laoghaire and well on our way to Bray. There's no speedometer in the cab, and the only way to find out exactly how fast we're going is to ask Mr Moore, the driver. He shrugs vaguely: 'Oooh . . . well . . . that'd be around thirty-five, I suppose.'

This is quite disappointing, and frankly alarming when I remember that some steam engines used regularly to hit 100 miles an hour. *Mallard* once made 126.

'She's only a goods engine, you know. Small wheels. Forty's the limit.'

After a while I start feeling guilty about enjoying the sea view while alongside me fathers of twelve-year-old football finalists are shifting some of the five tons of coal that's needed to keep us going. I offer my services and am soon entrusted with the vital task of raking the coal forward on the tender so it will slide more easily down towards the fireman's shovel. I'm provided with a long steel hook, which I fling with great difficulty on to the coal, dragging it towards me, grunting with effort and generally getting in everyone's way. Make a mental note never to write about the beauty of manual labour again.

With the last of the fairgrounds and promenades behind us there is a steady climb up to Bray Head, where a single stack of rock separates the line from a 200-foot (61-m) drop to the waves below. Mr. Moore helpfully points out a precipitous ledge ahead of us.

'Can you see there, Michael? That's where the line fell into the sea!'

There isn't much chance of an extended conversation on the footplate, which is perhaps why railways never really caught on in Ireland. When everything has to be shouted against the din of speed, communication becomes like Morse code.

'Now!'

'More?'

'Full!'

'Half.'

'Steady.'

'Stop!'

'Two!'

'Ease off!'

And that's just ordering a cup of tea.

We pass through a series of tunnels. This is a terrific time to be on the footplate. With no artificial light available, we're plunged instantly from sunlight into pitch darkness. Confined within the narrow walls, the smoke swirls and the noise from the locomotive booms and reverberates. To provide light the driver pushes open the doors of the firebox and the crew bend to their work in the flickering glow like figures from some revolutionary tableau.

After this heady excitement we settle to a long run along the coast, during which time I'm taught the rudiments of firing. Swinging coal from the tender into the narrow aperture leading to the boiler is one of those things that has to be done right. Not in three shuffling movements but in one flowing turn, at the end of which the coal must be delivered not only cleanly but precisely on to the spot where the fire most needs it. Balance and timing are much more important than brute strength. Fred Astaire would have made a wonderful fireman.

In the foothills of the Wicklow Mountains, winding unhurriedly through enchanting valleys, the line is single-track, and spreading bushes and overhanging trees crowd the cab, making leaning out a hazardous business. At times it feels as if we are the first train to come down here for a hundred years, but I'm told there are six passenger trains a day between Dublin and Wexford as well as three chemical trains. *Chemical trains!* Here in Paradise?

My romantic illusions prove non-sustainable, as red discoloration appears on the rocks and oily smears taint the previously clear water of the streams. Almost unbelievably we turn a corner and there is a large ammonia-processing plant. Apparently it is all connected with by-products from the natural gas fields discovered off the Cork coast. As oil exploration has not produced much, the Irish economy needs all it can get from natural gas, even at the expense of the unspoilt beauty of the Avoca Valley.

From Arklow, the line runs inland between low hills and along the course of the River Slaney until it crosses flat, estuary scenery to meet the sea again at the ancient town of Wexford. Ancient and lively by the sound of things. It hosts an annual Opera Festival and a Mussel Festival and has its own bull-ring. I've hit it at the wrong time of year for the festivals, and there hasn't been a bull seen near the ring for two hundred years, but I do get to meet the Mayor and the Pipe Band. Unfortunately I'm still in my overalls, and the Mayor and his retinue bustle past me looking for Michael Palin. Eventually he's persuaded that this oil-stained figure is the man they've been expecting and a short civic reception is organized in the guard's van, complete with speeches of welcome. A small, dark-haired lady who is the Mayor of Wexford's twin town in France looks bemused but smiles bravely as I'm presented with a leather-covered edition of a poem specially commissioned from local man Tony O'Sullivan. It's entitled 'The 7.20 a.m. Wexford to Rosslare, A Poetical Evocation':

> Pulsating carbon-black sleek
> iron-skinned steed whose

clanking hooves will soon
hammer the drum tattoos of
metal sound into predawn
tracks . . .

A short train ride from Wexford, except on Sundays, is the town of Waterford, self-proclaimed 'Shopping Capital of the South-East', founded by the Vikings in 853 as Vadrefiord. It was about the only Irish town of any size to have peacefully survived Cromwellian occupation. It seems pleasant enough, even though the guide books do say the best view of it is from Mount Misery.

Away from cosmopolitan Dublin an Englishman is faced with some uncomfortable realities. The Union Jack can still not be flown here, even though we are now European partners. I saw a caravan park with every major Western flag flying apart from my own. This is not accompanied by any open hostility, for though anti-Englishness will always remain tucked into the Irish psyche, it is never allowed to get in the way of hospitality. This I enjoyed from various quite different sources. One was from a band of motorcycle enthusiasts who have opened their own bar, the Hogshead, on the waterfront. South-east Ireland is, for reasons none of them could satisfactorily explain, a sort of spiritual home for bikers. My informant, Swifty, is a Waterford bus driver in love with Harley-Davidsons. One of his friends sports an Electra Glide originally owned by Sid Vicious. Eamonn, who runs the pub, is more vexed by a recent visit from the police who ordered him to remove his condom-vending machine from the toilets. He is apparently allowed to sell them over the counter, but not from the machine. Though Swifty and his friends speak with almost religious fervour about the great international confraternity of bikers there are clearly some nearer home who let the side down. Swifty can hardly bear to speak the name of the Road Tramps of Limerick. 'They're the worst,' he mutters, with the sort of feeling for his fellow Irish that Cromwell would have been proud of.

For another view of south-east Ireland I undertake a short pilgrimage down the coast towards Cork, an area no longer served by the railway. This is a shame as, among the lazy curving bays and the long beaches sheltering below sharply angled cliffs, there are places worth seeking out. There is the village of An Rinn, where I first come across the sign 'Gaeltacht', which means Gaelic-speaking community. A little further on is largely unspoilt (provided you don't count the caravan park) Ardmore. Here, untrumpeted, are the extensive remains of an 800-year-old cathedral. The medieval wall carvings are as unexpected as they are unforgettable. Carrying on up the hill I come to a house with a sensational bay view where lives one of my favourite Irish writers, Molly Keane. She's in her late eighties, physically frail but captivating company, and enjoying an Indian summer of popularity. When I arrive she's full of enthusiasm for the cover proof of an anthology of Irish literature she's just put together.

'Very good, don't you think? This dark bit here . . . captures the malign side of Ireland . . . Ireland,' she says, 'has bred two writers that were almost Tolstoy, and that was Somerville and Ross. *A Real Charlotte* is terrifically good, and they wrote that, two virgin ladies in 1890.'

When I ask her to confirm my impression of a country on the up she is very sceptical. There is much less respect for law and order. She herself was robbed quite recently; friends have suffered too. I ask her if she thinks things are worse now than when she was a young girl in Dublin.

'Oh, greatly.'

There seem so many conflicting views amongst the Irish about the Irish. The 'malign side', as Molly called it, always seems to lurk close by, running alongside the warmth and the amiability, a fatal contradiction ready to counter all the best things about the Irish – Yeats's 'terrible beauty'. Why these things should preoccupy me, almost personally, is maybe the confirmation of the power of the Gallagher gene. I'm now on the edge of Gallagher–Watson country, and a letter has just arrived from my genealogist in Dublin giving me a tighter focus for my search – around the town of Mallow, about 60 miles to the west.

The railway doesn't run directly from Waterford to Mallow, so I take a three-coach local, pulled by a diesel locomotive, along the Blackwater valley, a fine salmon-fishing river flowing through comfortable, fertile farming land. This takes me to Limerick Junction Station, which is two miles from Tipperary and twenty miles from Limerick. Don't ask me why it isn't called Tipperary Junction.

There is nothing there when I arrive save a station plonked down in a flat, featureless plain beside a rickety old racecourse. Flies chase each other about the platform, which stretches for a quarter of a mile.

'Longest in Ireland,' I'm informed by a lethargic railwayman.

In the fresh cement of some recent resurfacing work someone has scrawled: 'Paddy You Made a Bollix of This'. The place lacks glamour. Until, that is, the arrival of the Cork express. At last a proper train, hauled in effortlessly by a 2750 horsepower diesel (there is no main-line electrification in Ireland) made in the USA by General Electric. It can cover the 160 miles between Dublin and Cork in 140 minutes. But the real pride of the lines is City Gold, 'The New 21st Century Rail Service'.

City Gold service comes with a lot of seat-side technology and brochures full of words like 'ergonomics' and 'bulkhead data displays'. Before you can lie back and start snoring you have to undergo a sort of aptitude test. Mine is undertaken, whilst the longest platform in Ireland slowly recedes, by Fiona, who has been trained by Aer Lingus for such tasks. The nub of Fiona's gist is that I am not just sitting on a more than averagely comfortable railway seat, I am sitting, ergonomically soundly, at the very frontier of communications technology. I have the use of not one, but two, telephone points at my table. I can phone, I can fax, I can choose a selection of tapes and CDs to play on my personal stereo headset, I can summon Fiona at any moment, I can adjust my seat, I can probably launch a tactical nuclear missile if I find the right button. And all this for only 15 punts more than the normal fare.

This technological glitz impresses me less than the fact that fares on Irish Intercity are half those of the UK *and* they take bicycles. And they stop at Mallow.

It's ironic that my swiftest and most cosseted ride on any Irish train should last less than half an hour. They want to make it faster still, driven on doubtless by the desire to achieve some respectable showing in the Euro-speed stakes. They've quite some way to go, with the French and Germans reaching for absurd speeds of 200 miles an hour. Who wants to travel along the ground at 200 miles an hour? Rail travel was surely never intended to be a test of G-forces.

Mallow is a world away from such preoccupations – a pleasant, relaxed agricultural town on the Blackwater River. The station has an old unfussy cast-iron canopy from which sky-blue paint is peeling, and palm trees in tubs on the platform. A goods train rattles through carrying anhydrous ammonia from the gasfields near Kinsale.

Ten miles north of Mallow I begin my Gallagher search at the village of Buttevant, where I've been told there is a local man-who-knows-everything by the name of Tony O'Neill. Tony runs a grocery shop in the main street, as his father did before him and his grandfather before that. And his children after him? I ask.

'No, they've too many brains,' says Tony, indicating that I should come round to the back of the shop.

At the back of the shop is a bar, as incongruous as the two petrol pumps at the front. In between nipping round the partition to sell sliced bread, Tony pulls me a Guinness and begins to elaborate on the local Gallaghers. Gallagher was originally O'Gallagher . . . did I know that?

No, I didn't know that.

And they came from Donegal . . . Which is more or less where I started my journey.

Tony ponders this one. On the other hand, if Brita was

orphaned and sent to America she would almost certainly have left from Cork, or more likely Tralee.

The country network then goes into action, and on Tony's advice I find myself driving across to the nearby village of Doneraile to a place known locally as 'Tommo's Bar' where I'm to ask for a man called Niall who knows more about Gallaghers even than Tony. Niall turns out to be ill with the flu, but his wife, who is minding the bar, says she's sure he won't mind talking to us. The only problem is that they don't live here, they live in Buttevant. Drive back to Buttevant where Niall dons bedroom slippers, comes downstairs and, despite all my protestations, insists on ringing his friend called Gallagher. There is no answer. He then reduces ancestor-hunting to basics, opening up the phone book and calling every Gallagher he can find. This elaborate networking eventually bears fruit in the shape of a man who can authoritatively state, over a Guinness, that there were indeed Gallaghers who emigrated from Buttevant in the nineteenth century. Unfortunately they left about forty years after Brita and went to Australia.

I'm beginning to lose heart. It seems that the closer you get to the centre the further everything drifts away. The trail has led me to 1880s Australia and left me there. Everyone's terribly helpful, though, and won't hear of my giving up. Next morning I learn that a nest of Gallaghers has been located in the graveyard at Glanworth – a village some 20 miles away. The local school has conveniently produced a catalogue of all the headstones and in it are listed no fewer than ten Gallaghers, and, at last, some who date back to the time of Brita's birth in 1844. An Edmond Gallagher and his son William were living here in the early nineteenth century. Only two of the ten graves are those of women – one Ellie, one Annie. Either could have been my great-great-grandmother, but I'm frustratingly short of proof.

It's only city-dwellers who expect time to stand still in the country, and when I return to Tony O'Neill's bar for consolation I find Tony busy playing host to the competitors in a road bowling competition. This seems a very Irish sport, though I'm told that it was originally brought into the country three hundred years ago by the Dutch soldiers of William of Orange. Basically all that is required is a road, four throwers and a 28-ounce (0.8-kg) cast-iron ball. Each team has two men whose aim is to get this dangerous missile to the end of a three-mile stretch of road in as few throws as possible. If you happen to be returning from a quiet day's motoring you could be in for a shock, as the ball can easily be thrown 300 yards (274 metres) and, with a ricochet and spin off the tarmac, could go as far as a quarter of a mile. It's not recommended for the M25, but on the quiet lanes outside Buttevant, with a crowd of supporters straggling along in the pink glow of the setting sun, this unruly sport takes on a timeless quality, as bets are laid on each throw and the spectators noisily break ranks to let through the odd perilously-balanced trailer piled high with straw.

I've almost run out of railway and I've almost run out of clues to the origins of Brita Gallagher, but I decide to play a last hunch. It will take me to the shores of the Atlantic Ocean, on which Brita would, at some as yet unknown time, have been borne across to America.

Back to Mallow, only this time to pick up not City Gold but country grey – three coaches in search of a cleaner, which wend their way to the head of the Blackwater and into the bolder mountain scenery of the indisputably beautiful county of Kerry.

Tralee is where my wife and I spent the second night of our honeymoon, twenty-seven years ago. There was so little to do that we went to bed at eight. About quarter past a chamber-boy let himself in and, putting on the light, was about to turn down the counterpane when he saw us beneath it, leaped several feet and bolted for the door. This time I don't even bother to check in before taking my very last train of the journey, along the recently restored mile or so of the old Tralee and Dingle Light Railway, to Blennerville, now Ireland's most westerly station, and a hundred and fifty years ago one of the great emigration ports.

Was this little hamlet, dominated by the sweeping slopes of

the Slieve Mish mountains, with its unmistakable windmill and stout stone bridge, my great-grandmother's last view of her country? It certainly was for many thousands of victims of the Great Famine. Between 1845 and 1851 over one and a half million people left Ireland – 18 per cent of the total population. How might she have travelled? On deck, unfed and unprotected, with those who had paid ten shillings for a passage to New York? In a dark, insanitary hold where men, women and children slept together for a month or more? Perhaps even in some luxury, paid for by a rich family friend already in America?

There is a smart new visitor centre at Blennerville a hundred yards away from the crumbling old jetty where the emigrants once queued to board. Here they try to answer some questions about the extraordinary trauma of the famine years and the Irish diaspora that followed it. They have several of the old passenger lists which give in some detail the name, age, sex and occupation of those who left. I could find no mention of a Gallagher, let alone a Brita Gallagher. The records are far from complete – she could have been aboard the *Heather Bell*, left for New York 1849, passengers unknown, the *Jeanie Johnston*, left for New York 1850, passengers unknown, '3 Large Ships', left 1851, passengers unknown. She could have left from Cork or even Derry.

The only encouragement in all this confusion is that the Irish themselves want to know what happened to almost a quarter of their ancestors who upped and left in the nineteenth century. No country can lose so many and not want to account for such a loss. I take the little train back across the marshes, now part of a reclamation scheme with Leisure Parks and WaterWorlds set to replace the mud and the Tralee Council tip. Though I've finished a railway journey of nearly 650 miles I feel I've only just started another journey. One that will only end when my Irish curiosity is satisfied.

CAPE TOWN TO THE LOST CITY

Rian Malan

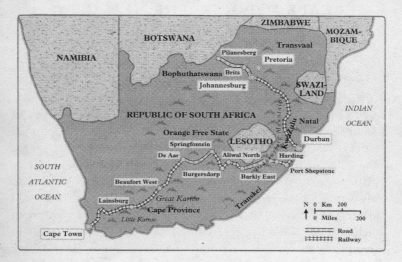

Rian Malan's journey from Cape Town to the Lost City

Oi! Alors! This is more like it – escape from the miseries of South Africa aboard a luxury steam train, a thousand US dollars a ticket from Cape Town to Jo'burg and free champagne all the way. Yes, thank you, I'll drink to that. I'm standing on a railway platform at the foot of Table Mountain, quaffing bubbles with my fellow passengers – a judge, a handful of stockbrokers and arbitrageurs from Jo'burg and sundry well-heeled foreigners, including the immaculately coiffed Mrs Patricia Stevenson of Evergreen, Colorado. I am feeling rather light-headed, having consumed immoderate quantities of champagne at an unaccustomed hour, so I pose a cruel riddle to the posh American, certain that she'll say something foolish.

It concerns two trains. On this platform we have a string of immaculately restored 1920s coaches, painted in the green livery of Rovos Rail and hauled by a magnificent steam engine. The corridors are panelled with mahogany. The lamps are Tiffany. The doorknobs are great chunks of burnished brass. There's a comfortable double bed in the corner of each compartment, a picture window framed by chintz, a bottle of Pierre Jourdan chilling in a silver ice-bucket on the table. On the platform adjoining we have the grubby 9.15 from Khayelitsha, now

Since the 1994 election in South Africa the bantustans Bophuthatswana, Transkei and KwaZulu have ceased to exist.

disgorging a load of ragged black commuters from the poverty-stricken shack communities out on the windswept salt flats. So tell me, Mrs Stevenson: which of these trains is the true South Africa?

She reflects for a moment, then comes up with an answer that surprises me. 'What is significant,' she says, 'is that they exist side-by-side.' She's a wise woman, Mrs Stevenson. She believes that God may have sent her here to ameliorate South Africa's sufferings, and all I can say is thank you, because we need all the help we can get.

And now it's *toot-toot*, all aboard, and the luxury train pulls out of the station and into a dismal industrial wasteland. I watch from a window as Table Mountain falls away behind us. In due course the landscape changes, factories giving way to vineyards, gracious gabled homesteads overhung by oak trees, a white horse rearing in a lush green meadow, purple mountains rearing behind. It's a very lovely landscape, in a kitschy, Swiss chocolate-box way. So gentle, so civilized, so un-South African. The Cape has never seemed quite real to me. In fact, this train doesn't seem real, either. There are amazing luxuries on the menu – smoked salmon, Parma ham, crayfish mayonnaise – and a truly intoxicating selection of fine Cape wines. I share a bottle of Buitenverwachting Buiten Blanc with Mrs Stevenson, who cheerfully notes the presence in her wineglass of a tiny fleck of soot from the engine. Ah, yes, the ancient glories of steam travel.

After lunch, I recline on my double bed and watch the passing spectacle through my chintz-framed compartment window. We're racing along the banks of the Hex River now. Dark mountains loom ahead, the odd shaft of sunlight falling on their flanks, their jagged spires lost in cloud. The land is growing drier now, harsher, more African. The train winds up to the head of the valley and burrows into the maw of a long tunnel. We're in total darkness for nine minutes, and then *wham*, the train blasts out into an arena of sun and stone, where nothing moves save the shadow of clouds, drifting slowly across the sun-blackened plain.

This is the Moordenaar's Karroo, the Murderers' Karroo, a semi-desert where early travellers perished of thirst between waterholes. It was once the hunting ground of Bushmen, and the summer pasture of nomadic Khoi. There were vast herds of game, and locust swarms so huge and dense that the earth grew dark beneath them. These days there's the occasional lonely old farmhouse, flanked by a clanking windmill and bluegum trees, but mostly there's nothing – just rocks and dust and pulverizing heat. I love this landscape, so arid and gaunt and empty, all illusion burnt off by the heat. I want to take my clothes off and walk away in it. I am so tired of despair, this horrible grey fungus on my psyche.

May I cry on your shoulder, and tell you about the New South Africa? It began on 10 February 1990, the day the prison doors swung open and Nelson Mandela walked free. The liberation movements were legalized, the guerrillas came home, the nation was momentarily drunk on euphoria. Everything was supposed to be different beyond that point, but everything somehow remained the same, save for the talks – talks about peace, talks about a new constitution, talks about talks, always more talks, endless, pointless and ultimately incomprehensible.

Meanwhile, there was terror in the townships, a series of fratricidal wars that claimed more black lives in a month or two than all the martyrs of apartheid put together. South Africans grew numb to the sight of burning houses and burning people. The violence undermined the economy, which started collapsing, and then the rains failed, and food prices rose to cruelly high levels. Things were getting worse instead of better. You began to yearn for the darkest days of apartheid, because then at least you could live in anticipation of miracles – a miraculous change of heart on the part of the Boers, a relaxation of repression, the repeal of laws that insulted and humiliated black people. Now all these things had come to pass, but they had not brought salvation. They had just carried us to the brink of an abyss.

It yawned open last Saturday, when a white assassin shot Chris Hani, beloved leader of the South African Communist

Party and one of the few grown men capable of controlling the ravening young lions of the ANC's Youth League. Within the hour angry clouds started building over Table Mountain, and by nightfall the worst storm in decades was raging, snapping trees, tearing the roofs off houses, hurling 60-foot waves on to the shore of False Bay. Yesterday the sun reappeared, and the young lions of our dark satellites came into white Cape Town and trashed it – a hand grenade here, a dead cop there, a row of small shops on fire. They kicked an old white man half to death. They attacked the ANC's shadow Minister of Finance. They threw a demobbed ANC soldier up against a tree-trunk and threatened to cut his throat because of his white skin.

At one point I saw the good Archbishop Tutu standing on the back of a truck, trying desperately to calm the surging crowd. 'I am the conductor here,' he shouted. 'Follow me! We shall all be free! Black and white together! Come on! I want to see your hands! We shall all be free! Black and white together!' About a third of the throng picked up the chant and love seemed about to triumph, but *blam, blam, blam*, the cops opened fire on looters and the crowd streamed away, screaming, leaving the road behind mysteriously strewn with empty shoes. The good Archbishop bowed his head. They took him by the arm and led him away, past a backdrop of boiling smoke and orange flames and armoured police vehicles, and I was left thinking, okay, this is it, the problems of South Africa have deteriorated beyond all hope of solution.

It was not a good thought to live with, so I was very glad to leave Cape Town, to board a train that carried me out into this arena of silent stone where white clouds march on for ever across the burnt brown land. I pull down the window and stick my head out into the slipstream. The hot wind sears my face like sandpaper, cracks like pistols around my ears. After a while I feel better. Maybe it's not so bad as I imagine, but what would I really know?

I live in Cape Town, a whites-only moonbase on Africa. I get up in the morning, read the newspapers, stare at a computer screen all day. I don't go to the townships much any more, because such excursions have become dangerous, and most of my friends are blind white mice, just like me. Which is why I'm pleased to be on a train, rolling north into the turbulent aftermath of the Hani assassination in search of . . . what exactly? Ten years ago, I might have come looking for cracks in the granite façade of apartheid. Three years ago, for tender green sprouts of democracy. In April 1993 I'm willing to settle for almost anything: a little hope, a little laughter, a little respite from this numbing sense of doom.

Beaufort West, 7p.m. Wave goodbye to the rich folk, sit down on a bench to await my connection. The sun sets, darkness falls, and policemen start gathering behind me — fat ones, thin ones, black and white uniformed constables, and cowboys in boots and riot gear. What's happening? I ask the captain. No, he says, there's trouble coming, a cavalcade of five trains full of angry mourners bound for Chris Hani's funeral, thundering towards us across the dark Karroo, ransacking every station *en route* for all we know. The captain is a bit tense. He thinks there may be ructions. I think, oh shit, here we go again.

In a while a yellow headlight appears in the distance, and a lonesome siren sounds out on the dark plains. A train comes sweeping around a long bend and into the station, scores of comrades hanging out of the windows, fists in the air, shouting, 'Viva ANC people! Viva! Viva!' They're clearly expecting to be met by revolutionary masses, but there's nobody but me and the cops and about ten youths in Muslim *topis* down at the far end of the platform. Everyone looks a bit embarrassed — the cops, the comrades, even me. God, what a pleasant anti-climax. Maybe this crisis is blowing over.

A whistle blows, the train jerks into motion, and I decide to go for a stroll around Beaufort West, founded in 1820, 'the capital of the Great Karroo'. It's what Afrikaners call a *rydorp*, a country town with broad avenues, roadside irrigation furrows and old tin-roofed houses with filigree cast-iron embellishments on the stoep and under the eaves.

On main street, three young girls are standing in a pool of neon outside a furniture shop, peering at the goodies through the window. They smile and start hustling me in Afrikaans: it's Saturday night, they're on their way to a disco but can't afford the entrance fee, so don't I feel like dancing? This one's Sharifa, she's Anita, and the one in hot pants is Biba. And how old are you? 'Nineteen,' they chorus, but I'd swear they're still in high school.

On the other hand, they're coloured people, descendants of the Khoi whose land this once was and wandering Boers who took it away from them − my own flesh and blood, in other words, but spurned by apartheid in my father's time, banished from white schools and white neighbourhoods, humiliated at every turn. The least I can do is buy them a night on the town.

So we set off walking down the Great North Road, the N2 highway linking Cape Town and Jo'burg, past a big white church, past the Engen Station and Ye Olde Thatch Hotel. We cross a dry river bed, and the lights of the white town fall away behind us. I say: 'Hey, what's this, where are you taking me?' The girls point to a floodlit building on the brink of a dark and empty immensity: Club Lipstick, the only disco in 300 miles.

Party-bent youngsters travel all day to be here. They park their old Toyotas outside, pay 3 rand (60p) at the glass booth, submit to the standard guns-and-knives bouncers pat-down and dance through into the throbbing interior. I'm not sure what I was expecting, but not this utterly bland normality: hundreds of clean-cut coloured kids wearing jeans and baseball caps on backwards, dancing to Michael Jackson under a battery of strobes. It could be any suburb, anywhere, save that everyone speaks Afrikaans. I move to the bar, and no, Biba, I will *not* buy you a beer. Schoolgirls drink lemonade.

I'm the only white here, but everyone is very friendly. Young men pump my hand, ask where I come from and where I'm going. Biba and Anita try to drag me on to the dance floor, but I'm too old to cut the funk in such sharp company, so I just prop up the bar and chat.

'What do you want to be when you grow up, Sharifa?'

'You'll laugh if I tell you.'

'No, I won't.'

'Okay – I want to be an air hostess. But I'm too short and too ugly. I wish I was whiter, like my sister. Then it would be easier.'

Poor Sharifa. She's clearly in pain on this score, so I bellow some encouragement in her ear – 'Don't talk nonsense, sweetheart: you're lovely to look at, lucky to be black. South African Airways is trying to catch up with the twentieth century! All they're hiring is black girls!'

Sharifa's face falls, and I realize I've put my foot in it. 'Do you really think I'm black?' she says. 'Do I look black? I'm not black. I hate blacks.' She launches into a long tirade about black people and their real and imagined shortcomings, all delivered with such passion that I am left shaking my head in bewilderment.

I mean, this girl's grandfather is a sheep shearer, slaving for a pittance on some white man's farm. Her father is a hopeless drunkard, his spirit crushed by apartheid. Her life is an unending struggle against poverty and racism, but she still thinks it's an insult to be called black. And there are plenty of Sharifas; 70 per cent of coloured people share her views to some extent or another, according to opinion polls, and support the Afrikaner Nationalists who imposed apartheid on them. 'Huh,' snorts Sharifa. 'Who is Mandela? He wants to take over, and then you'll see. No, I stand with the whites.'

Do I understand this? Not really. I just kiss my pretty little racist friends goodbye and head back for the station.

Beaufort West to De Aar: five hours on the Trans-Karroo Express. This is a different train, a government train, with green vinyl upholstery and speckled green formica panels along the corridors. Coloured 'bed boys' bustle up and down the corridors, taking orders for bedding. The conductor squints at his passenger list, trying to divine the race of passengers due to board at the next station. This is a tricky business. There's no more racial discrimination on South African trains, but old habits die hard;

conductors still try to put whites and blacks in separate compartments 'just to keep the peace'. Hence the conductor's racial
guessing game. Mavundla is definitely African – put him with
Motlana and Mabaso. Van de Merwe is probably an Afrikaner,
so give him his own compartment. Smith, on the other hand –
Smith is problematic. Could be English. Could be coloured.
Could even be a Boer, pronounced 'smit' to rhyme with 'snit'.

As it turns out, the Smith on tonight's train is a retired
schoolteacher from Riverlea, near Johannesburg. He and his old
friend Mr Kling are sitting opposite me in the dining car,
tucking into bowls of soup. They're solid, balding, middle-class
men in grey slacks, short-sleeved polyester shirts and sensible
shoes. They've been travelling on trains all their lives, but this is
the first meal they've ever eaten in a first-class dining car because
they happen to be coloured. Prior to 1988, coloureds weren't
allowed in here. They had to ride up at the front of the train,
where soot from the steam engine came in the window and got
between your teeth and in your eyes. They had to drink cold
coffee from leaky cups bought from the tuck-shop for second-
and third-class passengers. And yet here they are, sipping whisky
and soda from crystal glasses, tucking into a three-course meal
that way surpasses anything you'd get on a train in, say, Canada.

Mr Smith has a sister in Canada. 'You know,' he says, 'she
phoned the other day, when she saw all the Chris Hani violence
on TV. She said, "Get out of there, it's turning into an inferno."
And I say, "No, you're wrong. It's a whole new world. Everything is better these days. Better than it used to be."'

I ask how it used to be, and Messrs Smith and Kling tell a few
stories. 'Once upon a time,' says Mr Kling, 'I was driving
through the Orange Free State and I overtook a farmer in a
pick-up. He chased me down and said, "*Jou blerrie Hotnot, hoe
durf jy 'n wit man oorsteek?*" (You bloody Hottentot, how dare
you pass a white man?] And then he made me drive behind him
all the way to the border, on pain of a serious beating. Ha-ha-ha.
But it's over now, it's history. We must forget the past. We
must give credit where credit is due.'

'Once upon a time,' says Mr Smith, 'I played in a multi-racial cricket game – some coloureds, some Indians, a few blacks and a white or two. Afterwards, we went to a shebeen for a drink and got caught up in a police raid. The cops said, "*Jerre*, how can this be, Hottentots and kaffirs and coolies all drinking together? You're under arrest." Ha-ha-ha. We were schoolteachers, and we were so worried for our jobs, man. Ha-ha-ha. But that sort of thing doesn't happen any more, thank God. Our grand-children don't believe it.'

Mr Smith is worried about the youth of the country, the black youth, because some of them are poisoned with hatred. Look at these Chris Hani riots. It's terrible. Shocking. Shameful. He thinks hatred is bad. He understands it, because he also suffered under apartheid, but he fights against it because he's a Christian, an Anglican. 'We mustn't dwell on the past,' he says.

For instance, we mustn't dwell on the bad old days when young coloured men like Mr Smith were relegated to coloureds-only rugby leagues which played on sloping, rocky fields with bluegum poles as goalposts. 'My friend here was one of the best fly-halfs ever,' says Mr Kling. 'Everyone who saw him said so. He could have been one of the greats, but he was coloured, so the best he ever got was a Mickey Mouse Transvaal Coloured cap.'

Mr Smith howls with laughter. 'Ja,' he says. 'But everything is different today. Now when I go to rugby I sit in the glass box with all the bigwigs from the Union. We've got a coloured boy in the Springbok team. They even sent me overseas as a dignitary. It's a completely different world. But I tell you one thing,' he says, leaning forward across the table suddenly deadly serious, 'I will never cheer for a Springbok team. Never. Because I could have been there myself, but they never gave me a chance, because I was coloured.'

He was just like my father, that man, a solid, sensible, middle-class citizen, concerned about church affairs and pension schemes, insurance and rugby. My father had all the chances that came with a white skin, and he used them to vote for apartheid, for the system that kicked Mr Smith in the face. I wonder what my old man would say if he was sitting here, in this rattling dining car, enjoying a post-prandial Cape brandy with these two fine coloured men. I think he'd have to say, 'I'm so sorry, Mr Smith; so sorry, so sorry.'

Next stop, De Aar. God, what can I tell you about De Aar? It takes its name from a giant river that nobody has ever seen, because it runs underground. It owes its existence to a huge railway junction, the biggest in South Africa.

A funny thing happened in De Aar: we missed our train by six weeks or so. It had been cancelled for lack of passengers, the men who ran it transferred or pushed into premature retirement. The vast, sprawling station was eerily silent and empty. In the shunting yard workers were cutting up old steam engines with blow-torches, like Norwegians flensing a dead whale, while desperately poor unfortunates scrabbled in the dirt nearby for old buried bits of coal. It was all rather dismaying.

So how then to reach Springfontein, 200 miles away? There was nothing for it but to hitch-hike. I stood on the road with my thumb in the air until a ten-ton truck stopped for me. 'What's going on here?' I asked the driver, an old Boer named Mr Van Zyl.

'The railways is buggered,' said Mr Van Zyl.

'Why?' said I.

He just shrugged. 'I don't know,' he said. 'Something's wrong, I suppose.'

I'll say. There were no long-haul railways in South Africa until gold and diamonds were discovered in the interior. Then the race was on – four different heads of steel snaking inland from harbours to the goldfields. By 1900 the major towns and cities were connected, and then the spaces between were filled in, creating a railway network dense as the veins in a body. South African Railways grew larger and larger until it was a state within a state, with its own army, its own police force, its own hospitals and schools and factories, and a vast, bloated workforce of 280,000, about a third of whom were white, holding skilled jobs reserved by law for whites only, and earning salaries commensurate with their pigmentation.

Working on the railways was a very sweet job for a white man. The pay was poor in comparison with the private sector, but the SAR cradled you in its arms and cared for you like a mother. You got a house in the railway colony for next to nothing, with free water and electricity. You got subsidized loans, subsidized higher education, subsidized beer and bioscope at clubs known as Railway Institutes. Nobody ever got their arse kicked. Nobody was ever fired. The train bosses moved great loads of dead air up and down the country, just so their mates could claim overtime. The railways were supposed to operate at a profit, but that was just a clause in some law. Nobody ever worried about it. The massive losses were just entered in a dusty ledger in Pretoria and forgotten.

This continued until the late seventies, when the apartheid state began to come under withering pressure from several quarters. Black pirate taxi-men were openly defying the state's claimed right to control public transportation. White-owned trucking concerns were clamouring for the freedom to carry freight wherever they pleased, in open competition with the railways.

Our government was very arrogant in those days, but the pressure was relentless, and in the end it had to back down. In 1985 or thereabouts, the government abandoned its attempt to monpolize public transport and legalized the black taxi industry. Forty-six per cent of black commuters promptly deserted state-run transport for taxis. Something similar happened a few years later, when the state unshackled highway truckers: the railways turned out to be far too fat and slack to survive in the marketplace. Within months the truckers had grabbed a huge share of the freight market, and the railways were bleeding. The SAR shed a hundred thousand jobs in the next five years. Unprofitable lines were shut down, unprofitable stations abandoned. The entire railway system seemed to be collapsing, with devastating consequences for small towns like Springfontein, on the outskirts of which Mr Van Zyl had just dropped me.

Springfontein was founded in 1904, at the junction of four railway lines. The station was its lifeblood, its *raison d'être*. Once upon a time the freight yard was full to overflowing with clanging shorties and bogies, but now it's virtually empty. There are only four trains a day, only sixteen jobs at the station – down from almost two hundred in 1967. The broad main road is silent save for the cooing of doves in bluegum trees. A third of the shops are standing empty, festooned with 'For Sale' signs. The town's only bar is a mausoleum. The white school has closed, and the old railway barracks has been bricked up and abandoned. There's no one in sight save for a sad old Boer, bleakly contemplating two perky ostriches in his back yard.

His name is Flip Nel and he's a railway worker, like everyone in Springfontein is or used to be. He started as a labourer and worked his way up to shunter at Springfontein Station. He never earned much money, never saved any of it, and now he's facing imminent early retirement or retrenchment. 'They could tell me tomorrow, "Mr Nel, you have to go on pension," and I'll tell you honestly, I have no insurances. No savings. I used that money to live on. That's why I bought this place.'

He gestures at the smallholding over his shoulder – about two acres of land (just less than a hectare), now lying fallow. Until a year or so ago he had a small farm here – sold eggs and vegetables to blacks from the township, even kept a milk cow. Things were going rather well until this foolish De Klerk fellow let Nelson Mandela out of jail. 'Since then,' he says, 'there's been nothing but trouble.' His 'boys' went on strike over low wages (60p a day) and never came back. Blacks stopped buying his produce, preferring to patronize black traders.

In desperation he bought a breeding pair of ostriches, having heard that a single fertile ostrich egg would bring $1000 in the United States if you were cunning enough to smuggle it there. He put them in his back yard, bought several sacks of ostrich food and sat back, counting dollars in the pipeline. But the male ostrich turned out to be gay or something, totally uninterested in getting his leg over. He just stands in the sun all day, eating and preening himself. Mr Nel falls silent and glares at the offending bird. I say, '*Ja-nee*,' a Boer expression which translates as yes/no and comes in handy when there is nothing else to say.

Poor old Flip Nel. There's an element of poetic justice in this tale, I suppose, but it's hard not to feel some sympathy for a man buried so deeply under the rubble of collapsing expectations. Everything in his life is disintegrating – his railway, his *volk*, his *vaderland*, his comfortable assumptions about white supremacy and his ostrich-breeding scheme. 'What will become of us?' he sighs. 'That is the question. What's to become of the white man?'

What indeed? Springfontein seemed as good a place as any to ponder the matter – on the northern rim of the Great Karroo, thirty miles shy of the Orange River, almost midway between Cape Point and the Zimbabwe border. If South Africa was a disc, a pin through Springfontein is the axis around which it would spin. It's also a model apartheid town, its various 'population groups' separated from each other by a broad *cordon sanitaire* of open veld, in accordance with what was once assumed to be the law of God and nature. In the east lies the Bantu location, where blacks live in dire poverty in tiny, overcrowded houses. In the west, on the far side of the railway line, lies the coloured township, where the houses are a bit bigger. And in the south lies the white town proper, a pretty little place with broad dirt roads and bluegum trees and old tin-roofed houses, clustered around the station and the Dutch Reformed church spire. As of 1993 the population was 250 whites, 500 coloureds and 9000 Africans, with only 400 jobs to share between them.

Will democracy take root in such poor soil? I stroll into Springfontein's only supermarket and put the question to Stef Venter, the white town's mayor. He says 'Well, maybe.' There's no violence in Springfontein. Everyone is negotiating. The coloureds and whites have formed a single municipality, and relations with the ANC-controlled township are cordial. Unemployment is a terrible problem, and blacks are unhappy about a certain white policeman, a bully by reputation; but otherwise, Stef is quite happy. 'I tell you,' he says, 'I just wish we could cut this town off from the rest of the country, because we can make it work here. We get on well with our blacks here. We grew up on the farms with them. We know how they think.'

Oh, really? I've heard that line a thousand times before, usually from rural racists who have absolutely no inkling of how blacks feel. So I walk across the train line and into the black township where I bounce Stef's opinions off Andrew Mantyiani, the local ANC leader. Andrew started life as a garden boy, earning 60p a month in the late sixties. Later he became a truck driver on the railways, earning one Rand where the average white man earned four. Irked by these and other injustices, he joined the ANC underground and ultimately left the country for military training. Mantyiani fought in the epic battle at Cuito Carnavale in Angola, where the Boers got a bloody nose. In 1991, he came back to Springfontein and lit a fire under Stef Venter. There were some rough patches at the outset, a bitter consumer boycott and some unruly demonstrations, but there's been peace for the past two years apart from a brief episode of tyre-burning on the night of the Hani assassination. Stef runs the white town, the ANC runs the township, and if problems crop up, Stef and Andrew sort them out together.

In fact, I got the impression that they actually liked each other, the Boer mayor and ANC ex-guerrilla. Stef was more or less reconciled to the fact that he would lose power in a one-person one-vote election, and he seemed to regard Mantyiani as an acceptable heir in spite of the hammer and sickle flying over his headquarters. Mantyiani was a revolutionary, to be sure, but capable of appointing an Afrikaner to run the township's high school because the white man was the best candidate. Mantyiani was also a Marxist by conviction, but his dreams of a new Springfontein sounded curiously Thatcherian to me – a factory here, a co-op there, tax incentives to lure foreign investors and a canal to bring water from the river, so his hungry people could grow some food. He was totally uninterested in vengeance.

'We're not going to fight the whites,' he said. 'We love these people. We grew up with them. We used to milk their cows.'

I was quite taken aback by all this, I must tell you. It was the last thing I expected to encounter in the Deep South of the Orange Free State, whites and blacks more or less at peace with each other, and graffiti on the township soccer stadium reading, 'Please, Africans, don't be foolish; don't kill.' I wouldn't swear that Springfontein was bound for a happy ending, because both leaders were under pressure from extremists in their own camps, and Springfontein could still erupt in ethnic cleansing if negotiations broke down at the national level. Still, there was a foundation, there was something to build on. I saw the light of hope in Springfontein, but it dimmed over the next several days.

It's 3 a.m. on a cold, wet morning, and I'm standing on the platform at Burgersdorp Station. The Amatola Express brought me here from Springfontein, and now I'm all alone. The station is silent and deserted. There's nowhere to buy coffee. The only sign of life is a soft light on a second-floor ceiling under which a lone railwayman turns out to be dozing at his desk. He comes to the window, tells me to stop complaining: in a month or two, the whole station will have closed down entirely.

I shout, 'So where's my train?'

'There,' he says.

'Where?'

'There!'

But it's not a train at all, just a single carriage sitting in an empty siding all on its own, waiting for a locomotive. Oh, well. I'm too tired to care. I just drag my bags aboard, crawl on to a bunk, cover my shivering extremities with a jacket and fall into a sleep so deep that I don't wake when the train starts moving. In fact I don't wake up until mid-morning, by which time there's green grass outside, and trees, and a river way off in the distance. We left the arid Karroo behind while I was sleeping.

This line is controlled by a company called North East Cape Rail. It peels off the main line at Burgersdorp and heads up into the foothills of the Drakensberg Mountains through Aliwal North and Lady Gray. It was built during some forgotten wool boom, then rendered redundant by tumbling commodity prices and the internal combustion engine. Rather than abandon it entirely, the state has leased the line to NEC Rail for 20p a year, steam locomotive included, to see if it can be made to work as a tourist attraction. There are two trains a week, carrying a little freight and the odd local passenger. For the most part, though, NEC Rail depends on holidaymakers. A group of American tourists was supposed to be aboard today, but they were unnerved by TV reports of violence and decided to stay on the far side of the planet. Which means, in effect, that I have the entire train to myself.

My very own steam train. It's like a *Boys' Own* fantasy. I can do whatever I want to do. I can hang off the side of the train, climb on the roof, dangle off the side in the slip stream. I can go up on the footplate and watch the stoker wielding his shovel like a rapier, *shoosh* into the base of the coal tender and *whoosh* through the iron door and into the molten red maw, every lump landing exactly where it's needed, and never a single lump split. It's an incredible sensation, to race across this open country in the belly of a fuming dinosaur, pistons churning and venting like the lungs of some leviathan. The driver pulls a string, the whistle screams. Sheep and cattle scatter in terror.

A brief halt at Lady Gray, where swarms of little black children gather to watch water pour into the hissing boilers, and then it's *toot-toot* and away into a landscape of reddish cliffs and broken hills, slashed by steep watercourses. Farms and barns huddle in the lee of hills, sheltered from the wind by lines of poplar trees. Willows weep over clear, cold trout streams. I'm standing in the open door of the caboose with Antonie the brakeman, trying to spot trout in the deep green pools.

Thunk, screech. The train grinds to a halt, nose-to-nose with the rock face at the head of a canyon. Antonie jumps out, throws the points, and the train backs out on a second line, running a bit higher than the one we came in on. It reverses all the way over the river and across the valley and into another defile, where the procedure is repeated – Antonie jumps out, throws the points, and the train lurches forward on a line running parallel to but a little higher than the one we came in on. The gradient is too steep to be tackled head-on and too broken for tunnels or bridges, so the train sort of zigs and zags its way up the mountainside, climbing a little higher on each reverse. If you were watching from a distance through a time-lapse camera, we'd appear to be waltzing. I love it. Waltzing into the Drakensberg on a steam train.

Next stop Barkly East, and we're in another adventure. Barkly East is on the edge, no doubt about it; a dingy, mean town under a cold, grey sky, acrid smoke drifting in from the overcrowded, tumble-down township. Sullen black youths line the dusty main street, their eyes tracking two cops driving back and forth past them in a yellow van. It's as if these kids are watching a tennis game. I ask one of them, 'What's happening?'

No answer, just a long, cold stare. He eventually says, 'Where you from?'

I say 'Cape Town.' I wait for him to continue, but nothing comes, so I try again. 'What's happening here?'

The boy says, 'You know.'

Well, yes, I suppose I do. We're in the Eastern Cape now, one of the most tense corners in this troubled country. The land hereabouts once belonged to the Xhosa tribe. They lost it to whites in a series of ugly wars in the 1840s and 1850s, but now the tide of history is turning and whites are beginning to come under pressure. Cattle rustling is rampant. Several isolated farmers have been murdered by APLA, the Azanian People's Liberation Army, a shadowy black power outfit dedicated to cleansing the countryside of settlers. In response, farmers are erecting electric fences and floodlights, laying trip wires linked to home-made mines. A disturbing number have joined the AWB, the neo-Nazi Afrikaner Resistance Movement, and as for the blacks, they're gravitating towards APLA, if local graffiti is anything to go by. So yes, 'bru, I know what's going on here; you guys seem to be heading for a bout of ethnic cleansing, and I doubt that anyone can do anything about it, save wring hands and pray.

Myself, I lift up mine eyes unto the mountains, the jagged peaks of the Drakensberg, moody and grey today, shrouded by cloud. That's where I'm going, way up to the top and down the other side, but how to get there? The train line ends in Barkly East. There are no buses, no car hire companies, and the road beyond this point is a bucking, boulder-strewn abomination, requiring a really tough truck. I spot a suitable conveyance outside Barkly East's only hotel, and next thing I'm roaring up the mountain pass in a police Casspir, one of those grim armoured personnel carriers that gained worldwide notoriety in the mid-eighties, when apartheid repression was the top story on TV news.

A Casspir weighs eleven tons (11,176 kg). It's bullet-proof, bomb-proof, mine-proof, invulnerable to almost everything save nuclear attack. I've seen these babes rumbling through riot-torn townships, blasts of tear-smoke and birdshot emanating from their portholes, but I've never been inside one before, and never met anyone quite like Warrant Officer Murdoch. I was half-expecting a bloodthirsty white savage, but he's a genuinely nice guy, a diesel mechanic or 'nutsman' by specialization. His unit was sent here four months ago, to patrol these lonely roads against APLA. So what's it like? I ask. Cold, he says. Bloody boring and cold.

An hour later, we're up among the crags, suspended in white light and thin air. The morning's cloud has vanished, and the land falls away below us in a breathtaking tumble of steep stone cliffs and green plateaux. The last farmhouse has fallen away far behind us, and now there is nothing from horizon to horizon save gaunt brown mountains and wind-bent bushes and icy rivulets alive with the silver flash of feeding rainbows. It's so lovely it leaves you gasping, makes you want to stand in the road and shout ecstatic nonsense at the sky for the uncontainable and unbearable ecstasy of it, but what would the policeman say? More to the point, what will Officer Murdoch make of Ernest Oelofse, towards whose farm we are heading?

Ernest and I go back a long way – back to the very first Bruce Springsteen record, in fact: 'Greetings from Asbury Park', 1973 or '74, featuring lyrics of this approximate order: 'With my black leather jacket and hair slicked sweet/Silver star studs on my duds like a Harley in heat . . .' and so forth. Ernest thought it was about him, but then he also thought he was Hunter S. Thompson and Hemingway, with a liberal dash of Trekboer: a legend in his own mind, in other words. 'I'm into courage,' he once told me. 'Courage for courage's sake. Courage because I'm a man.'

Ernest is the only man I ever met who could say things like that and not be laughed at. He was lean and mean in boots and jeans, and he had all these passions that didn't fit in a city – hunting, fishing, fighting cocks from Puerto Rico and a body that rejected the suit and tie. He was a journalist when I met him, working for the liberal *Rand Daily Mail*, but he got bust for dope and rendered himself unemployable.

After that he had a go at novel-writing, but the novel never got beyond the first ten pages, and in the end he tired of that too, so he loaded his dogs and his guns in the back of a truck and set off for the wilderness to be a free man. The general idea was to find a place so remote that no one could follow – beyond fear, beyond guilt, beyond the reach of cops, taxmen, army call-ups, feminists, animal rights activists and bandits with AK47s. He thought he'd found it in these mountains.

Rural etiquette dictates that I invite Officer Murdoch to join Ernest and me for some refreshment, but he has better things to do, luckily. He drops me on the main road, and I walk the rest of the way, over hills, through fences, down dales. Round one last bend and there it is – an old stone cottage, straight out of Thomas Hardy, nestling in the valley far below hollyhocks in the garden, shaded by oaks; no electricity, no running water, and several broken windows where the winter snow drifts in. The name of the farm is Shepherd's Hope.

It's dusk by now and dark by the time I barge in through the kitchen door, scattering ducks and chickens. Ernest is trying to pick up the news on a hissing, sputtering portable radio. His wife Janice is bathing baby Joseph in an old tin tub in the glow of a hurricane lamp. There are dogs underfoot, cats everywhere, chickens pecking in dark corners. A stew is simmering on the old wood stove. There's a 9mm pistol on the kitchen table, and alongside it, a whisky bottle, already open in anticipation of this reunion.

It's Janice's turn to cook supper, so Ernie and I sink a whisky or two over the backgammon board and do some catching up between games. He came up here to escape the great storm bearing down on white South Africa, but instead, he seems to have wound up in the thick of it. The area is crawling with policemen, trundling up and down the track to Shepherd's Hope in their Casspirs. Almost all his white neighbours have become paramilitary loonies. Just over the ridge lies the Transkei, tribal homeland of the Xhosa people, now infested with bandits and APLA terrorists.

This is bad news for Ernest, who makes his living running sheep and moonshine whisky into the Transkei for resale. Two years ago, each trip was a lark, but now, it's nerve-racking. Ernest was stabbed the other day in an attempted hold-up. Several whites he knows have been shot at, at least three murdered in ambushes in the past week or two. Ernie's into courage for courage's sake, but even he's getting scared.

'It's funny,' he says, 'my father always said, I want you to be better than me, and I always thought that was middle-class bullshit, because, I mean, better — what is better? Better is relative. It was the day I had my own kid when I realized. I was riding into the Transkei with a pistol in my belt and a shotgun between my knees and my eyes peeled for an ambush, and I thought shit, I don't want my son *ever* to have to do this. You know what I mean?'

I do, 'bru, I do, and on top of that it hasn't rained all year and the sheep get rustled on moonlit nights and the farm is far too small to support Ernest's family plus fourteen assorted serfs and freeloading Rastafarians. His situation is actually quite desperate, but he refuses to give up and come back to the city. 'Bugger it,' he says, 'I love it here.' I say, 'Let's drink to that,' and by 2 a.m., the whisky bottle is dead.

The next day was a very bad day. I staggered to my feet at 10 a.m. and borrowed a pair of shades to shield my brain from the merciless sunlight that stabbed through my eyes like daggers. Janice helped me into the front seat of the bakkie, the pick-up, and Ernest drove me all the way down the mountains and across the Transkei to the town of Harding, where I had a train to catch.

There's a train waiting in Harding Station, a curious narrow-gauge job, loaded to the gunwales with wattle logs and reeking creosote poles. I slosh through mud wallows and hail the driver, whose name is Dawie. He says, 'Sure, come on,' and I haul my bags up a steel ladder and into the warm cab of the diesel, which smells of cigarettes and coffee. A blast on the horn and we're off downhill, heading for Port Shepstone, 77 miles and 4000 feet (1219 metres) below. There's a huge tree branch lying across the tracks, torn down by last night's storm. Dawie just smashes right through it. Big strong things, trains.

For the first hour or so we're travelling through thickets of wattle and bluegum plantation, looping and winding down the crests of the ridges like a puff adder. It's a very tricky line, this, so steep and serpentine that the locomotive often slows to walking pace, so there's plenty of time for talking.

Dawie has been driving this line for seventeen years. When he started there were up to eighteen trains a day, carrying timber and sugar cane down to the coast, but most of the freight was eventually lost to the roads, thanks to the SAR's stupidity and mismanagement. 'If they'd brought diesel in here in the sixties,' he says, 'they would have carried twice as much freight for half the cost and this line would have run at 100 per cent profit. We told them but they wouldn't listen. They never listen to the little man.'

So the line went bang and was about to close when it was rescued by an unlikely coalition of train buffs and business men, who saw a potential profit in timber and tourists. They renamed it the Alfred County Railway and it's doing fairly well now, moving timber down the mountains and carrying huge trainloads of happy holiday-makers around the coastal hills on the Banana Express steam train.

After a while, fences vanish from the countryside and flocks of ragged little black boys appear at the trackside, jumping up and down, waving, trying to outrun the train. We've entered the Murchison District, the southernmost fragment of KwaZulu, homeland of South Africa's largest tribe. The hills are dotted about with thatched mud huts, each standing on a platform cut into the mountainside, with a little patch of pumpkins and mealies nearby, and maybe a cow or a sheep tethered to a stake. Most of the homelands are hellholes, but this one looks idyllic to me – a landscape of steep green hills covered by waving elephant grass, the valleys between choked with fever trees and bamboo thickets, and on the horizon the startling deep blue sea. I spot a lovely pink house on a lonely hilltop, overwhelmed by flowering bougainvillea, and I think, 'Geez, I'd give anything to live in a place like that.'

But then again, maybe I wouldn't, because I'd have to cope with the *dlame*, an untranslatable Zulu term implying the violent disintegration of the world as known. The *dlame* arose from tensions between rural Zulu traditionalists, who supported the institution of chieftaincy, and urban Zulu socialists, who supported Nelson Mandela's ANC. At the outset the conflict was ideological, but it turned violent in 1986 and eventually blossomed into an ugly civil war in which around nine thousand Zulus have lost their lives and another hundred thousand have been rendered homeless. Here and there we see charred patches of land, each marking the site of a homestead burnt to the ground in the troubles. There was some heavy fighting in this district, but it came to an end six weeks ago, when local witch doctors warned that the killing of Zulu by Zulu and brother by brother was causing turmoil in the spirit world. They organized a ceremony in which many cattle were sacrificed to appease the ancestors, and there has since been peace in these hills.

Peace among Zulus, at any rate. The other war – the low-key struggle between settlers and natives – continues unabated. Today, the natives have placed a boulder on the track up ahead. Dawie doesn't flinch, just bears down upon it and crushes it. 'Happens almost every day,' he says. 'It's ironic,' he goes on. 'We bring water for them all summer. If it wasn't for us they'd die of thirst, but they still put boulders on the track, change the points, throw stones.' That's why Dawie has a gun in his armpit. That's why there's a security guard riding shotgun on the far end of the train. As if on cue, a tiny boy picks up a pebble and hurls it at the train, but he's so small that the gesture strikes me as funny rather than threatening.

I ask Dawie, 'Is this sport or war?'

He laughs and says, 'A bit of both, I suppose.'

Another hour down the line lies Izingolweni, where I say goodbye to Dawie and hop aboard the Banana Express for the run down to the sea. It's a lovely old colonial train, drawn by a gleaming red steam engine, buffed and polished to blinding perfection. Today it's full of steam buffs from England, obsessives and fanatics with only one thing on their minds.

'I say, George, isn't that a Garratt NGG16a, with the unusual twin-boiler configuration?'

'By jove, you're right! It's the 1953 model, made in Manchester . . .'

I pull a jacket over my head, and sleep off the hangover.

Ah, Port Shepstone, Port Shepstone, caressed by warm breezes, shaded by palms, swooning in a subtropical trance on the shores of the Indian Ocean. At last I get a hot shower, the first in days, and also a solid fix of hot news. I haven't seen a paper since Cape Town.

Aha. The martyred Chris Hani has been buried amid ongoing violence. A troika of alleged conspirators has been arrested in connection with his assassination – a Pole, an Englishman, and the Englishman's wife, an Australian. What an extraordinary plot – three outlanders conspiring to knock off a beloved Communist leader in a desperate bid to save white South Africa from black rule. Alas, the manifold ironies are lost upon ANC youth leaders, who refuse to drop 'Kill the Boers' from their repertoire of war songs and slogans. In response, four retired Boer generals have formed an Afrikaner National Front, sworn to forge unity among the fractious crazies and two-bit Hitlers of the white far right. The only good news comes from the World Trade Centre near Johannesburg, where the men in navy-blue suits have reconvened around the negotiating table, racing against the clock to hammer out an election date before the country slides into irredeemable chaos. So, yeah, it's a straw, but I clutch at it, and fall asleep in a good mood.

And now: dawn at Kelso Station, sky delicate pinkish to blueing, a brisk breeze stirring the palm fronds and bamboo, and the Indian Ocean black and heaving just below the station, so close they get spray on the tracks in a heavy storm. The train pulls out at 6.10 and runs north along the coast towards Durban, skirting blue lagoons and banana plantations, crossing rivers with magical Zulu names – Umzimkulu, Umbilo, Amanzimtoti. The hills to my left are clad in lush green sugar cane, while on the right I see mile after mile of golden beach, empty at this hour save for dogs and their walkers, and skiboats ramping through the breakers in explosions of spume. Far out to sea, under a line of orange clouds, I spy steamers bound for Zanzibar or Madagascar or Bombay.

As we draw nearer to Durban, the coach begins to fill up – black schoolgirls in black gymslips, white girls in brown ones, all in sensible shoes. They sit side by side on moulded plastic benches, bright yellow, scuffed and begrimed but still pleasing to the eye. At one station, several maids board the train. At the next, it's a man with a live chicken in a milk crate, and then two tiny Zulu boys, heads shaven bald and shiny, shivering with excitement about visiting the big city. Golden light floods in through the window, bounces off the yellow benches, suffuses the entire carriage with a golden yellow glow.

The sun rises a little higher, and then the first tall buildings appear, followed by industrial plants and refineries, and finally a forest of skyscrapers. The train burrows in under them and halts at Berea Station. We're in Durban, the largest port in Africa.

I pick up my bags and join a throng of commuters streaming into a long dark tunnel. The sound of a distant tumult reaches my ears. It grows louder and louder until it's deafening. One last staircase, and then, *wham*, the heat hits you in the face, and you stagger under the wild assault of bright colours and loud noises and exotic smells. You're standing on a concrete walkway, looking down on this teeming African marketplace. Every square inch of pavement is taken up by hawkers' tables and fruit stands, and every inch between is packed with people, one solid mass of sweating brown flesh, pullulating to the sound of ten different musics, all blasting simultaneously from quaking speakers – jazz in one ear, township jive in the other, reggae bass rising up through your feet. It's intoxicating. I strip off my jacket and wander around the throng, dazed, making lists of things I see . . .

Bananas, pawpaws, pineapples. Ivory carvings and gold chains. Pink patent medicines in old brandy bottles. Nduku Extra Power Number One hard-on pills. A Zulu Rasta in wraparound shades. Sweet potatoes and nectarines. Bras, beads, belts and combs. Hundreds of babies, crawling under tables. A woman with ten mattresses on her head. Silken saris from India, red, pink or blue. A pungent curry powder called Mother-in-Law Exterminator. A witch doctor, and then another. The healing and magical herbs of Africa: *mpepu* to guard against evil spirits, *umkhuhlu* to cleanse the system, *iphupho* to bring on prophetic dreams. Raw tobacco, Zambuck ointment and Tiger Balm. Bunny Chow and Samosas. A rich Indian in a big blue Mercedes, and finally a Zulu madonna, breast-feeding her baby under graffiti saying, 'Paul Simon go home.'

After a while I hail a passing tuk-tuk, or motorized rickshaw, and head off towards my hotel. The tumult of the marketplace dies away behind us and we enter a zone of generic Western banality – banks, insurance companies, post-modern architecture and Italian restaurants, and beyond that the Golden Mile, a strip of high-rise hotels lining the sea. I spent several holidays here in my boyhood, staying in a hotel called Marine Sands with Mom and Dad. I remember it as hot and crowded, infested with noisy holidaymakers from the hinterland, but it looks strangely subdued these days: empty shops, quiet hotels, only a handful of swimmers in the beachfront pools. When I sit down on the porch of the Balmoral Hotel, ten waiters in red fezzes step out of the shadows and offer to attend to my needs.

They're Indian, these waiters, Tamil-speaking descendants of indentured labourers brought to Natal in the 1860s to cut the sugar cane on which white Durban's prosperity was based. Most chose to stay here after their contracts expired, becoming a community of market gardeners, craftsmen and traders, widely reviled by whites as importers of infectious diseases, a bridgehead for nations trying to rid themselves of their superfluous population.

One of their leaders, towards the end of the nineteenth century, was a young lawyer named Mohandas K. Gandhi, brought out from Bombay to represent a rich Muslim merchant in a lawsuit. In June 1893 he was ordered off a train by a police constable, acting on complaints from whites who objected to sharing a compartment with a coolie. When Gandhi resisted, he was bodily seized and hurled on to the platform. It was an experience that changed his life, because it set him to thinking about the evil in the world and about ways of combating it.

He started reading Tolstoy and Ruskin, living according to the Hindu scriptures. A few years later he founded a utopian commune called Phoenix on a hillside outside Durban, where he and his followers lived in harmony with the land and with their Zulu neighbours. It was here that Gandhi formulated his philosophy of *satyagraha*, of truth and love as weapons in the struggle for justice, and here that he first put it into action in a series of campaigns against racial discrimination.

Gandhi returned to India in 1915 and went on to liberate his nation, but something of his legacy survived in Durban, and there was even a living Gandhi to show us around it – Mrs Ella Gandhi, the Mahatma's granddaughter. I had pleasant visions of this gracious Indian woman in a flowing sari strolling over lush green lawns in the shade of banyan trees, speaking lyrically of her grandfather's beliefs while the Hindu faithful burned incense and banged tambourines in the background.

So we picked her up one sunny Sunday morning and headed north along the coast. I assumed that the Phoenix Centre was in Phoenix, but we drove right past that placid Indian suburb and into a place called Bhambayi, at which point the sad truth was revealed. Gandhi's settlement had been engulfed by a vast sea of tin shanties, and then destroyed in a series of ugly fratricidal wars. First, the Indians were driven out of the area by rampaging Africans, their homes and shops burnt down behind them. After that, the area was ravaged by Zulu-v-Pondo tribal battles. The Pondos emerged victorious, only to split in turn into warring factions called the Reds and Greens, loosely synonymous with the ANC and the Communist Party. Sixty people had died in this phase of the war, while thousands had been burnt out of their homes. Both sides had retained the services of evil witch doctors and taken to gouging vital organs from the bodies of slain enemies for use in battle medicine brews. Bhambayi was very ugly. Bhambayi was the heart of darkness, and here we were in the centre of it, contemplating the ruins of Gandhi's settlement, burnt down in an anti-Indian pogrom seven years earlier. I was appalled. I turned to Mrs Gandhi and said, 'Is it safe to be here?'

She smiled and then she said, 'I was born here, so this would be a good place for me to die.'

This was not reassuring, but I steeled my nerves and we strolled around the ruins for a while, talking about the old days. These were the foundations of Gandhi's house. This was the outline of the porch where Ella had slept as a child. These ruins were once a library, and this burnt-out hulk once housed the press where Gandhi printed his newspaper, the *Indian Opinion*. Even the well from which his community of dreamers drew water was blocked up and abandoned.

'I think Gandhi would have understood,' said Ella. 'I think he would see that the African community has been deprived for a very long time, and that people's feelings do get agitated and difficult to control. I think Gandhi would say that we need to get together, rather than be afraid of each other. I think a lot depends on being prepared to share.'

I was willing to share almost anything at that point, just so long as we got out of there. On the way back to the city, though, I fell to thinking about what Ella had said, and making a few calculations. There are twenty-five thousand people in Bhambayi, all sharing a single tap. I have four taps in my house, which would make it five taps between us. I tried to imagine sharing a tap with five thousand other people, but it warped my mind so badly that I had to have a beer. There was piped muzak in the bar, Antarctic air conditioning, the glass chilled to icy perfection. It could have been any Holiday Inn in the white Western world, but it wasn't – it was the Durban Holiday Inn, just 15 miles away from Bhambayi, where 25,000 people shared one tap. This is the difference between white South Africa and the rest of the West; in South Africa you get to contemplate your selfishness in the face of other people's deprivation, and I tell you: it makes the beer taste flat.

Durban to Johannesburg, thirteen hours on the Trans-Natal Express, about £12 for a third-class ticket. This part of the train is full of poor black people, among whom I feel mildly paranoid and utterly alienated. The true languages of this country are African – Nguni, Sotho, Tswana and their many sub-dialects – and I speak none of them. I just gape at my fellow passengers, and try to guess what they're saying. Could be talking about the weather. Could even be talking about whitey, and what the hell's he doing down at our end of the train? I clear my throat and say, 'Sorry, but are you talking about me?' The question provokes gales of laughter.

'No,' chuckles Nomavenda Mathiane. 'She says my handbag is going to fall apart unless I get somebody to apply some glue.'

Nomavenda is a journalist, or at least she used to be. Then she wrote a book called *Diary of Troubled Times* and became a superstar, darling of anti-apartheid conferences in distant world capitals where people want to know what black South Africans were thinking. She usually jets from place to place. She's only here because she likes sparring with me, and because she's scarcely been on a train since her schooldays.

'I'm just thinking how nostalgic this is,' she says. 'There'd be eight of us girls, going off to school by train, and the boys would be lurking around and trying to get into the compartment.'

'And you fought them off, naturally.'

Nomavenda laughs. When she laughs, it's like the sun is shining. She says, 'Naturally.'

The conversation switches back into Zulu, and I stare out of the window. Durban is like a creamy chocolate – white and sweet at the centre, dark and bitter on the outside. The entire city is ringed by violence-ridden shack settlements, home to two million desperately poor Zulus who live in mud houses and tin shanties – no sewerage, no services, no jobs, no hope, almost no food. Countrywide, about eight million people are in similar straits, and Nomavenda says it's all my fault, or the fault of apartheid at any rate. I beg to differ, and in an instant we're sparring.

'What do you mean?' she hoots. 'I can't blame it on the regime? Don't talk absolute bloody rubbish!'

We've had this argument a thousand times before. Nomavenda says blacks are poor because of apartheid, not because they're stupid or lazy. I say, 'Sure, that's true, but the removal of apartheid won't necessarily change that. The price of bread won't drop when Mandela becomes State President. Millions of jobs won't suddenly materialize.'

Nomavenda says, 'You don't understand what I'm saying!'

I say, 'I do.'

'You don't!'

'I do!'

Those of our fellow travellers who speak English are nodding their heads, agreeing with Nomavenda: 'A vote isn't enough on its own. You can't eat a vote. You can't dress your children in it. The whole system must be changed!'

And I say, 'So what does that mean? Another Marxist–Leninist experiment? The whole world will laugh at us!'

Another exchange or two, and the conversation ends as it always does: in reluctant agreement. Nomavenda gestures at the passing squatter camps. 'There are many people out there,' she says, 'who think the vote is going to deliver bread, who think the vote is going to deliver houses. As soon as they get disillusioned they will do something. The problems and violence will continue.'

I cover my face and groan at this prospect. Nomavenda pats my shoulder, consolingly.

Just then, something goes *blam* in the corridor. Everyone jumps. What was it – a gunshot? Nah, just a dropped tray, But you never know. You never know.

It's 7 a.m. and here we are in eGoli, the city of gold, commercial and industrial capital of South Africa, driving through downtown in a taxi. I grew up in this city, so it's full of ghosts for me. There's the medical centre where I was tortured by a dentist as a six-year-old. There's the old Stuttaford's building, where my mother bought me chocolates for being a good boy. And there's the shuttered hulk of His Majesty's Theatre, where I once saw Percy Sledge sing.

Percy Sledge was the thin end of the wedge, as far as the black reconquest of white Jo'burg was concerned. It was the summer of 1970, as I remember, and the newspapers were seething with controversy about the impending visit of this black American soulman. The white right said, 'Keep him out, he's black, his songs promote sensual barbarity.' The rest of us said, 'To hell with that, let's dance.' Sledge was eventually granted a visa subject to several absurd conditions. A section of the Carlton Hotel was to be cordoned off for his use. He and his sidemen had to eat in their rooms, and were forbidden to drink at the bar. They were allowed to perform at His Majesty's, but only after the theatre had been roped off into ethnic enclaves. Sledge just grinned through it. He must have had a very thick skin.

A few years later, the first blacks sneaked into cheap downtown flats. This was illegal, of course. If someone reported you, you were subject to arrest and prosecution, but black people were tired of being pushed around. They dug in their heels, fought back when the police tried to evict them. Soon, whole city blocks were black, and then all of downtown. After that, the black tide rolled up the ridge to Hillbrow, or the Bronx, as we used to call it – a cosmopolitan zone of high-rise tenements and coffee bars and nightclubs. By 1980 the whole of downtown Johannesburg was comfortably integrated, but that was just a passing stage. By 1990 it was as black as Lagos or Nairobi and the government was beginning to look foolish and impotent, clearly incapable of enforcing its own laws. So it took down the whites-only signs and surrendered. Africa had reclaimed South Africa's largest and richest city.

The Mariston is unequivocally in Africa; it is a high-rise apartment hotel in Joubert Park, overlooking the railway line. There were Africans hanging over the balconies of surrounding buildings, Africans trading on the pavement outside. In the lobby, I encountered a Sudanese in white pyjamas and two Ethiopian lab technicians handing out business cards. A glamorous woman from Côte d'Ivoire was arguing with the clerk at the reception desk, and the man alongside me turned out to be Zairean.

I was aware that doctors and professionals had been trekking to Johannesburg from elsewhere in Africa ever since the release of Mandela, but their numbers had shot up to an estimated forty thousand in the six months since I was last in the city. There were hotels and nightclubs where French was the lingua franca. There were plush suburbs where half the real estate transactions involved rich newcomers from north of the Equator. The Nigerians and French Africans had come for business deals, the Ethiopians for food. Angolans and Mozambicans were here to escape the wars, and as for Zaireans, the tyrant Mobutu had reduced their once-thriving economy to an Iron Age wasteland where computer analysts were expected to trade their services for salt fish.

It was odd to look at Jo'burg through their eyes. To me it seemed sad and depressing: 40 per cent of its manufacturing jobs lost in the recession, ceaseless political turmoil on the periphery, and the highest murder rate in the world. For the Mariston's French Africans it was the most exciting, romantic and optimistic city on the entire continent – the Manhattan of Africa, not exactly welcoming the huddled masses, but certainly offering catharses and epiphanies and opportunities unobtainable outside Europe or America.

I spent the afternoon wandering around the city, trying to see it through their eyes, and in a while I got an inkling. In my boyhood downtown Jo'burg was like the moon, cold and white and sterile; but now the concrete canyons were full of life and colour. Black traders had taken over the pavements, and the streets belonged to black taxi-men, tough guys in Japanese microbuses, with crowbars or .38s on their dashboards. Thugs loitered on corners, peering red-eyed into the miasma of exhaust smoke, their menace counterbalanced by cheerful Rastafarians and cool black grungers with orange hair. There were also Hare Krishnas, rural Zulus in purple cloaks and Senegalese in white robes, not to mention veiled Muslims, Chinese numbers runners and your choice of briskly striding business men: black, white, coloured or Indian, two-piece suit or three. It was a vision of South Africa as it might have been, or might still be, if we somehow avoid destroying each other in a race war.

The odds were about fifty–fifty, judging by the doom-laden tenor of that evening's TV news. There were minor disturbances all over the country, more grisly murders on outlying farms. An ANC leader appeared on screen, talking about the stalled peace talks. 'If there is no settlement by the end of the month,' he said, 'the crisis may spin out of control.'

Meanwhile, black high-school students were petrol-bombing government buildings and vehicles pursuant to something called Operation Barcelona Flames, a violent protest against examination fees. The government had already backed down and waived the fees entirely, but the young lions didn't seem to care. They were pushing ahead with Barcelona Flames. In fact, they were planning to march on Johannesburg tomorrow morning, fifty thousand of them. It promised to be yet another bloody day.

In the morning the streets were quiet, but there was an undercurrent of tension in the air. Radio 702 said the cops had thrown a 'cordon of steel' around the city. They were pulling the Barcelona Flamers off buses and trains, turning them back at the gates. Thus far none had made it into the city, but Johannesburgers weren't taking any chances, judging from the torrent of customers pouring into the Gun Exchange across the railway tracks from my hotel. I went down to see what was happening, and found customers lined up three deep at the counter. A few years ago they would all have been white, but today at least half were coloured or African. A dark-skinned yuppie wanted a Czechoslovakian shotgun with a twelve-shot magazine. 'It's out of stock,' said the owner, 'but I can get you one by the end of the week.'

The customer said, '*Ja*, but we'll be in the shit by then.'

Outside, the sky was full of yellow helicopters, and armoured cars were moving through the streets. I was heading back towards the Mariston when I smelled tear gas. Just ahead of me hundreds of heads were turning, staring up a dead-end street towards Doornfontein Station. About three hundred young Barcelona Flamers had somehow made it through the police cordon. They were doing the *toyi-toyi* war dance, chanting, 'Viva APLA!' and 'Bullet! Bullet!'. A squad of riot cops in Darth Vader helmets had them bottled up at the end of this cul-de-sac.

Heavily outgunned, the comrades retreated over a railway

bridge and on to the station, where they commandeered the first incoming train – a suburban commuter train, full of white schoolkids and housewives on shopping expeditions. By the time I reached the front line the coaches were rocking back and forth to the beat of a war dance and a thunderous chant of 'Kill the Boer!' All you could see through the windows was a tangle of black limbs and the odd white face, squashed into a corner, terrified.

The comrades wanted the train to roll, but the cops said, 'No way, it's going nowhere until all the whites are off it.' Neither side was willing to budge. They just stood there, black power and white power, neck tendons straining, screaming and spitting in each other's faces while earnest peace monitors held their hands in the air and tried to talk faster than the fuse burned.

It was all so stupid and ugly, so utterly pointless and incurable. I was twenty-two when I first saw blood spilt on Johannesburg's streets because of apartheid. It broke my heart, but now … I don't know. There have been too many demonstrations in the intervening years, too much violence, too much chaos, too many dead. I don't want to look at it any more. I don't want to see it, or think it, or talk about solutions, because I'm beginning to think there aren't any. I just want to turn my back and ride away across the sunbaked plains, to a place where you don't have to think at all.

Once upon a time there was a train to our final destination, but the passenger service has been discontinued and grass is growing over the station. So we just got in a car and drove there.

As we arrived, I saw something amazing: rain pouring down from a blazing blue sky, and a black man standing like a statue on a rocky cliff above a waterfall, arms outstretched, eyes closed, face tilted up to the raindrops. Who was he? Who knows. Maybe they paid him to stand there and add a touch of mystery to the landscape. Maybe he was just a fantasy. In the Lost City, anything could be true.

Once upon a time, according to my official Lost City press

kit, a lost tribe came wandering down from the north and established a great civilization in this verdant African valley. Art and music flourished, peace reigned, and life was unbearably sweet until a terrible earthquake destroyed the city. All that is left are these ancient, weathered ruins, rising from tawny savannah like the set of some wildly improbable Hollywood epic.

As you arrive, a turbaned Nubian in flowing robes steps forward to claim your car keys. The ruins rise behind him, a forest of crumbling minarets and spires and ancient copper domes. Another Nubian takes your luggage, leads you through the massive wooden gates and into the ancient stone palace where African princesses and oriental damsels wait to do your bidding. Bowing and scraping, they pass you on to yet another young Nubian, who leads you deeper into the ruins. The air is filled with the perfumes of Arabia. Water drips off ancient stone masonry. Rivers leap from the living rock and flow away into mysterious underground passages. You pass through a hall the size of a cathedral, where strangers from distant lands are taking their tea, and then a door opens before you and the bellboy says, 'Sir, your suite.'

He's about eighteen. This is his third week on the job, and he just loves it. He shows you how to work the TV, the safe, the wooden ceiling fan. He draws your attention to the silver bowl full of luscious fruits and chocolate bon-bons, the rich bathrobes in the closet, the French champagne in the mini-bar. He draws back the drapes and offers you a view of the valley below, alive with streams and waterfalls and dotted about with magical ruins – the Temple of Courage, the Gong of the Sun Lion – all lit by orange fire of flaming torches. A dark green lake lies at the foot of the valley, and all around, tawny hills rise into an amethyst evening sky. All this splendour and magnificence, and the bellboy's alone to display. He turns, bursting with pride, and says, 'Isn't it wonderful?'

Well, yes it is. I came willing to be facetious, but this spectacle defeats me; all the clever remarks I'd half-prepared now seem so blindingly obvious as to sound stupid. So, the truth then: the Palace of the Lost City is magnificent.

The Palace is a grand hotel, as you have no doubt gathered, completed last year at a cost of almost $300 million. It is situated in Bophuthatswana, 'place of the Tswanas', one of the tribal republics created by apartheid. Bophuthatswana is ruled by Chief Lucas Mangope, a stern authoritarian who locks up dissidents and speaks scornfully of Nelson Mandela. It is politically incorrect to speak approvingly of such a man, or of the resort hotels-cum-casinos that litter his medieval fiefdom, but I don't really care any more – things have come to such a pathetic pass in South Africa proper that Bophuthatswana is beginning to look good by comparison. Children go to school, this charming bellboy has a steady income, and nobody gets killed or machine-gunned or burnt alive.

And as for Sol Kerzner, the hotel magnate who built this pleasure palace, I take my hat off to him, loo. He's a shameless white capitalist in a country where capitalism is decidedly unfashionable, but at least he's practising his black arts here, and not in Europe or America, where most wealthy whites have long since smuggled their ill-gotten gains. In fact I am staggered by his courage, or the enormity of his folly, in spending almost $300 million on a hotel so lavish that only foreign tourists can keep it going, and they're too scared to come because of the violence. Oh well. At least the night is quiet. I fall asleep to the chirping of crickets, and in the morning treat myself to breakfast in bed: rich, strong coffee from Kenya, warm bread, smoked salmon, and the morning papers from Johannesburg, bearing – at last – some good news. There has been a breakthrough at the peace talks. Mandela's team has yielded on the question of federalism, De Klerk's team has withdrawn its demands for a minority veto. The path is finally clear for an election – South Africa's first democratic election – set to take place early next year. All the editorials are ecstatic. They say there's light beyond the present darkness, hope beyond despair. They say we're heading for a happy ending, in which all men become brothers under liberal democracy, and even the poorest of the poor have jobs and food. Hey, it sounds wonderful to me. Maybe it'll really happen. And maybe it's just a fantasy like this place.

Ten years ago, South Africa was a simple country. There were only two sides – good and evil, black and white – and only two major power blocs: the Afrikaner National Party, which stood for apartheid, and Mandela's ANC, which stood for justice and freedom. But . . . I don't know. Apartheid has turned the country into a giant heap of firewood, infested with armed crazies who are openly dismissive of the Mandela–De Klerk peace settlement. The radical Pan-Africanist Congress is still attacking whites, and growing more popular daily. More and more Afrikaners are defecting to the far right wing, buying weapons and muttering about civil war. Zulu tribalists are also beating war drums, and now Winnie Mandela is back in the fray, urging the ANC's young lions to reject her long-suffering husband as a sellout and restore the revolution's purity. I would blind my eyes rather than see this, and cut my tongue out rather than say it, but I can't even imagine a happy ending any more. I think we're in for fifty years of turmoil.

So, what the hell – why not make hay while the sun shines? I wander down to the Temple of Ruins, where a Nubian draped with amber jewellery hands me a pair of swimming trunks and an air-filled tube, and I am soon drifting away on the current, into a long dark tunnel. It's totally black in here. You sail over an underground waterfall, and then you're in freefall, howling with terror. An eternity later, the sun explodes above your head, and you splash down on a blue lagoon. Something goes *whoosh* inside a cliff behind you, and suddenly, a tall blue wave is bearing down upon you, foaming at its crest. It picks you up, turns you topsy-turvy and deposits you on a beach of pristine white sand, where lovely girls in bikinis sip daiquiris in the shade of palm trees. Ah, yes, the sweet white life in sunny South Africa. I wade ashore to enjoy whatever is left of it.

Postscript

This article was written in the southern winter of 1993, the worst of all recent times in South Africa. A newspaper poll taken in that period showed that 40 per cent of us thought the violence would continue for years yet, while another 30 per cent thought it would continue 'forever'. I was one of the latter. If peace was impossible in the former Yugoslavia, what hope had we, with our howling canyons of class division, our Himalayas of racial and ethnic antagonism? None at all, as far as I could see.

And so it was with some surprise that I found myself, just one year later, casting a vote in the first free election in a country upon which peace had recently and miraculously descended. The story of how we got there and what it meant has been told and retold elsewhere. All that remains to be said is that there was a silver lining in the darkness of 1993, and that I, blinded by hopelessness, failed to see it.